The iPod & iTunes PocketGuide

Second Edition

Christopher**Breen**

All the Secrets of the iPod, Pocket Sized.

Peachpit Press

The iPod & iTunes Pocket Guide, Second Edition
Christopher Breen

Peachpit Press
1249 Eighth Street
Berkeley, CA 94710
510/524-2178
800/283-9444
510/524-2221 (fax)

Find us on the Web at: www.peachpit.com
To report errors, please send a note to errata@peachpit.com

Peachpit is a division of Pearson Education

Project editor: Jim Akin
Copy editor: Kathy Simpson
Production editor: Connie Jeung-Mills
Compositor and Illustrator: Owen Wolfson
Indexer: Rebecca Plunkett
Cover design: Aren Howell
Cover photography: Peachpit Press
Interior design: Kim Scott, with Maureen Forys

ISBN 0-321-48614-5

9 8 7 6 5 4 3 2 1

Printed and bound in the United States of America

To my own little iBreen, Addie.

Acknowledgments

This book wouldn't be in your hands if not for the hard work and care of the following individuals.

At Peachpit Press: Cliff Colby (who edited a fair chunk of the first edition of the big ol' *Secrets of the iPod and iTunes* and proffered the original idea for an iPod book); Jim Akin, who edited this edition of this book; Kathy Simpson (who copyedited every version of the big book and stepped in as editor of the first edition of this guide to whisk it out the door with nary a glitch or bump); Rebecca Ross (who handled the contract negotiations with such aplomb); the three Nancys (Peterson, who edited the first five editions of SotiPaiT; Davis, who Gives Final Approval; and Ruenzel, who makes everything go 'round); Connie Jeung-Mills (who coordinated production of the book); Scott Cowlin (who is a book-selling machine); Owen Wolfson (who laid out the book's pages and created some new illustrations), and Rebecca Plunkett (who provided the index).

At home: My wife, Claire, who once again kept the other parts of our lives together while I applied nose to grindstone in the basement; and the boys of System 9 for being such groovy cats.

Abroad: Rick LePage and Jason Snell at *Macworld*, who, one fateful day, harmonized, "So ya like iPods, eh? Howzabout we pay you to do nothing but write about them for a year?"

And, of course, the designers behind the iPod and iTunes. They just get better and better!

Contents

Getting Started

While I admire your desire to learn more about your iPod by purchasing this little guide, my guess is that before you delve too deeply into this book, you'd like to actually use your iPod. That's what this chapter is for—getting you up and running as quickly as possible. Here are the steps to take:

1. Open the box.

   After you've ripped the wrapping off your iPod, try turning it on. If it recently came from the factory, it could be charged and nearly ready to play.

To switch on any iPod except the iPod shuffle, press and hold any of the iPod's buttons. (I have the best luck pressing the Center button in the middle of the click wheel.) If the iPod is charged, it should display an Apple logo after a few seconds and then be ready to roll in about 30 seconds. If nothing happens when you try to start the iPod, make sure that the Hold switch on the top isn't on. If you see any orange next to the switch, it means that the Hold switch is on. Slide the switch over to disengage it. If the iPod still won't start, it must be charged.

For the iPod shuffle, push the power switch to the right. If a light shows on the LED next to the switch (green or amber), the iPod is charged enough for you to play with it. If no light shows, it needs charging.

2. Charge it (if necessary).

If the iPod doesn't work out of the box, you need to charge it up. On an iPod with a display (any iPod except the iPod shuffle), you can do this by plugging the included USB cable into your computer's powered USB 2.0 port and plugging the other end of the cable into the bottom of the iPod. If you have a charger for your iPod (chargers are optional for all iPods), you can plug the cable's USB connector into the charger instead of your computer, the other end of the cable into your iPod, and the charger into a wall socket.

The iPod shuffle is charged from your computer's powered USB port via its included USB dock. Plug the dock into a powered USB port to charge the iPod.

3. Install iTunes.

If you don't already have a current copy of iTunes on your computer, download it from www.apple.com/itunes. (Apple no longer bundles a CD copy of iTunes with the iPod.) Follow whatever onscreen directions are necessary to put iTunes on your Windows PC or Mac.

4. Rip a CD.

No, don't actually rip the disc in half. *Rip* in this context mean to transfer the audio from the CD onto your computer. To do this, insert the disc into your computer's CD or DVD drive and launch iTunes (if it doesn't launch automatically after you've inserted the disc). By default, iTunes 7 and later tosses up a dialog box that reads "Would you like to import the CD *nameofCD* into your iTunes library?" (where *nameofCD* is the name of your CD). Click Yes, and iTunes will convert the audio files to a format that can be played on the iPod. Also, the tracks you ripped from the CD will appear in iTunes' main window when you click the Music entry in the iTunes Source list.

To import that CD at a later time, click No in this dialog box. Then, later, select the CD in the Source list, and click the Import CD button in the bottom-right corner of the iTunes window.

5. Plug in the iPod.

If it's not plugged in already, plug your iPod into your computer. With an iPod other than an iPod shuffle, this means stringing the included USB cable between a powered USB 2.0 port on the computer and the Dock Connector port on the bottom of the iPod. If you have a display-bearing iPod other than a nano or fifth-generation (5G) iPod, you can use an optional FireWire cable instead of the USB cable.

The second-generation (2G) iPod shuffle requires the dock that comes with it; just plug the dock's cable into a free USB 2.0 port. Original iPod shuffle models have a built-in USB connector that plugs directly into your computer.

After you plug in your iPod for the first time, a window will pop up, asking you to name your iPod. Feel free to accept or ignore Apple's invitation to register your iPod at this point.

If your computer is connected to the Internet, the iTunes Store window will open within the main iTunes window. Yes, Apple wants you to shop, but you don't have to.

If there's any music in your iTunes Library, iTunes will ask you whether you'd like to import album artwork for your iPod. Unless you have a dial-up connection to the Internet, let iTunes retrieve this artwork; it will make using your iPod and iTunes a more enjoyable experience (as you'll read later). If you have lots of tracks in your Library—more than a few thousand—retrieving that artwork can take a while.

iTunes will also seek out tracks that should be played gaplessly—music from albums like Pink Floyd's *The Dark Side of the Moon* or any number of classical recordings in which one track should flow seamlessly into another.

Although iTunes 7 and later can play music gaplessly, this feature is supported only on 5G iPods and 2G iPod nanos. All earlier iPods will play music with short gaps between tracks.

6. Transfer music to the iPod.

By default, the iPod is configured so that it updates its music library automatically when it's connected to your computer. The music you ripped from your CD should transfer quickly to the iPod. If it doesn't, simply choose File > Sync *The Name of Your iPod* (where *The Name of Your iPod* is... well, the name of your iPod).

7. Unmount and play.

When the music has finished transferring, locate the name of your iPod in iTunes' Source list, and click the little Eject icon next to it. When the iPod disappears from iTunes, unplug it from your computer.

Unwrap the earbuds that came with the iPod, jam them into your ears, and plug the other end into the iPod's Headphone port. On an iPod with a display, rotate your thumb around the wheel on the front until Shuffle Songs is selected, and press the iPod's Center button. On an iPod shuffle, just switch the iPod on by sliding the power switch to the On position and then pressing the Play button on the front of the shuffle.

To adjust the volume on a click-wheel iPod, rotate your thumb clockwise to increase volume and counterclockwise to turn it down. On a shuffle, press the + symbol on the top of the control ring to crank it up and the − symbol below to make it quieter.

8. Enjoy.

Meet the iPod

My guess is that you wouldn't be reading these words if an iPod weren't already part of your life— or soon to be part of your life. Congratulations. You've chosen to ally yourself with the world's most popular and—in my humble opinion—finest portable music player.

Oh, sure, there have been pretenders to the throne— countless "iPod killers" that, on closer examination, proved to be nothing more than less-capable and less-stylish wannabes. Despite multiple attempts to diminish its dominance, the iPod remains It— the music player to own.

And now that you do, it's time to become better acquainted with your musical buddy. To get started, let's take a tour through the various iPod models and rummage around in the iPod's box.

Today's iPods

The danger of slapping on a heading like "Today's iPods" in a book like this is that—given Apple's habit of revving the iPod line every 6 to 9 months—Today's iPods may be Yesterday's iPods by the time you read this. However, unless the next-generation iPods breathe fire and project high-definition movies, the iPod you own shouldn't be disturbingly different from what I'm writing about in the autumn of 2006. Here's the lineup.

Fifth-generation iPod (Late 2006)

Throughout this little guide, I may refer to this iPod (**FIGURE 1.1**) as the *fifth-generation (5G)* or *standard iPod* to differentiate it from the smaller iPod nano and iPod shuffle. To separate it from earlier standard iPods that were incapable of playing videos, I may also call it the *iPod with video*. I have to jump through these hoops because in October 2005, Apple bestowed video playback on all its standard iPods; later re-released the iPod U2 Special Edition (which is nothing more than a standard iPod with a colored click wheel and some scribbles on the back); and then, in September 2006, released an updated version of the 5G iPod called the fifth-generation iPod (Late 2006).

Figure 1.1 iPod.

Photo courtesy of
Apple Computer

The iPod is offered in three main configurations: the
$249 30 GB iPod, the $349 80 GB iPod, and that $279
30 GB iPod U2 Special Edition I mentioned earlier.
The 30 GB iPods hold around 7,500 4-minute songs
encoded in AAC format at 128 Kbps (don't worry—I'll
explain this whole encoding-and-Kbps thing in the
chapters devoted to iTunes). These iPods can also
hold up to 25,000 pictures (specifically formatted
for the iPod by iTunes) or up to 40 hours of video
encoded with Apple's H.264 video encoder at a resolution of 640 by 480 (again, I'll provide the ins and
outs of video encoding elsewhere in the book). The
80 GB iPod holds approximately 20,000 4-minute
songs or up to 100 hours of video encoded in these
same fashions. All these iPods store music and data
on an internal hard drive. The non-U2 models are
available in either black or white, whereas Bono's
favorite iPod can be had only in a black case with a
red click wheel.

In addition to playing music and videos, these iPods
can display pictures transferred from your computer
or from a digital camera using a compatible transfer

adapter. With the help of Apple's $19 iPod AV Cable,
these iPods can display videos and pictures as slideshows on a connected television or digital projector.
Like the second-generation (2G) iPod nano, the
standard iPod can record audio with the assistance
of a compatible microphone attachment, such as
Belkin's $70 TuneTalk Stereo for iPod with Video,
Griffin Technology's $60 iTalk Pro, or XtremeMac's
$60 MicroMemo. It can also play iPod-specific games
such as Tetris, Pac-Man, and Mahjong.

Like all iPods, this model is powered by a recharge-
able lithium-ion battery. Constant play time between
charges on these iPods varies depending on the
model you own. The 30 GB iPods play music for
around 14 hours or video for around 3-1/2 hours on
a single charge if you don't muck too much with
the iPod's controls and leave backlighting off. The
battery will last through about 5 hours of constant
use when you view pictures on the iPod's screen and
about 2 hours when the iPod displays pictures on a
connected television or through a projector. The 80
GB iPod has a higher-capacity SDRAM chip (which
the iPod uses for storing music loaded from its hard
drive) and so it provides greater play time on a single
charge—around 20 hours of music, 6-1/2 hours
of video, 6 hours of pictures shown on the iPod's
display, and 5 hours when showing slideshows on a
connected television. (In Chapter 7, I'll tell you how
to get the greatest life out of that battery charge.)
Although this iPod and the iPod nano can be charged
via either a FireWire or USB connection, they can sync
only over USB.

iPod nano (2G)

Figure 1.2
iPod nano.

Photo courtesy of
Apple Computer

The 2G iPod nano (**Figure 1.2**) can be silver, blue, green, pink, red, or black. It's colorful on the inside as well—though its color display can show only pictures and slideshows; no video. Like the standard iPod, the sleek nano bears a crisp and colorful display (1.5 inches rather than 2.5 inches) and sports a click-wheel control. Also like its larger siblings, it has a Dock connector on the bottom; unlike those larger iPods, it has the Headphone port on the bottom too. The Hold switch remains on the top.

Apple offers the nano in three main configurations: The $149 2 GB iPod nano, which comes only in silver; the $199 4 GB iPod nano, available in silver, green, blue, pink, and a (PRODUCT) RED Special Edition (for which $10 of the $199 price goes to the Global Fund to fight AIDS in Africa); and the $249 8 GB iPod nano, which comes in black only. The 2 GB model holds approximately 500 songs; the 4 GB, 1,000 songs; and the 4 GB nano, 2,000 songs. Each holds up to 25,000 pictures. Unlike the larger iPods, the iPod nano has no internal moving parts. Instead of a hard drive, it stores music and data on flash-media chips—solid-state storage circuitry. In addition to being tiny, these chips offer a singular advantage: They make playback skip-proof. Playback on a full-size iPod can skip if you're playing long or large tracks, or if you bounce around a lot, as you might while exercising. This isn't an issue with the nano, as music is fed immediately from the flash chip to the nano's amplifier. This makes the nano an ideal workout companion. The iPod shuffle uses this same flash media.

Battery life on the nano is more than what you get on the full-size iPods. Apple claims approximately 24 hours of music play time.

Although the nano supports picture viewing on the iPod, it won't project pictures to a television. Neither does it support picture storage or the iPod games sold at the iTunes Store. As with the standard iPod, if you'd like to charge your nano from a source other than your computer, you'll have to pay Apple $29 for the privilege, as a power adapter isn't included.

iPod shuffle (2G)

Figure 1.3
iPod shuffle.

Photo courtesy of
Apple Computer

This is Apple's "displayless iPod"—one that's about the size of a matchbox and that includes no screen to indicate what the iPod is playing. Unlike the other iPods, the iPod shuffle (**Figure 1.3**) has no Dock connector port. Instead, it sports a Headphone jack that also acts as a data syncing and power port. To sync and charge the shuffle, plug it into the included USB dock and then plug that dock into your computer's USB port. Although it has a controller in the shape of a wheel, the wheel doesn't spin; you simply press the wheel's outer ring to adjust volume and move from track to track (or to fast-forward or rewind through the currently playing track) and use the wheel's Center button to play or pause the shuffle.

The iPod shuffle can be had in a single $79 1 GB configuration, which holds approximately 240 songs. As I mentioned earlier, the shuffle uses flash memory rather than a hard drive, which makes it another good choice for the gym.

This iPod also has a lithium-ion battery (though it's very, very small). Apple rates constant play time between charges at around 12 hours for the shuffle.

Given the shuffle's price and size, you can understand that it has certain limitations. The lack of a display is the most obvious one. This is not the iPod to own if you want to find and play a specific track easily. Instead, you should think of the iPod shuffle as your personal radio station—one that you've programmed with your favorite music so that you won't care which song it plays.

Because it lacks a display, the shuffle doesn't hold pictures, contacts, calendars, and notes—which other iPod models can display. It can't record audio from an outside source, either. Also, it won't play tracks encoded in certain formats. It can play AAC, AIFF, MP3, and WAV files, but it won't play Apple Lossless files. (I'll discuss encoders and formats when we visit iTunes in Chapter 3.) The shuffle is exactly what it appears to be: a basic music player.

Phoning It In

When is an iPod not an iPod (and, therefore, worthy of nothing more than this small sidebar)? When it's a phone. Motorola was the first to release an iTunes-compatible mobile phone—the ill-fated ROKR. Why ill-fated? It was a little clunky looking; it took forever to sync music because of its USB 1.1 interface; and it held a scant 100 tracks. Motorola later released the SLVR, a sleeker phone, but it suffers the same 100-track limit and slow USB 1.1 data transfer rate.

Thinking Inside the Box

At one time, Apple stuffed the iPod box with loads of goodies: in-ear headphones; a couple of cables for transferring data between your computer and iPod; a power adapter; a Dock and case for more-expensive iPods; a belt clip for the iPod mini; a video cable for iPods with color screens; a software CD and documentation; and, of course, the iPod itself. Rummage around in the box of an iPod you've purchased in the past couple of months, and you'll find that a lot of these items are now missing and available only as $19 or $29 add-ons.

No worries—what is in the box provides you enough to get started. Here's what you'll find inside the iPod and iPod nano boxes.

Earbuds

Figure 1.4 The iPod's earbuds.

Your iPod comes with a set of headphones that you place inside—rather than over—your ears (**FIGURE 1.4**). Headphones of this style are known as *earbuds*. A pair of foam earbud covers accompanied earlier iPods; Apple now offers a new earbud design that lacks these disks.

Just as you'll find a wide range of foot and head sizes among groups of people, the size of the opening to the ear varies. The earbuds included with first-generation (1G) iPods were a little larger than other earbuds you may have seen. Some people (including your humble author) found these headphones uncomfortable. Later iPods included smaller earbuds that I found much more comfortable. I find that without the foam disks, the latest headphones don't fit my ears terribly well; they just won't stay in a position where I can hear the audio "sweet spot." If, like me, you find the earbuds unsatisfactory, you can purchase smaller or larger earbuds, or you can opt for a pair of over-the-ear headphones.

If the included earbuds do fit you, you may or may not be pleased with their performance. Apple made great efforts to create the finest music player on the planet, and it didn't skimp on the headphones, but sound is subjective, and you may find that other headphones deliver a more pleasing sound to your ears. If you believe you deserve better sound than your Apple earbuds provide, by all means audition other headphones.

USB 2.0 cable

The iPod's proprietary Dock connector (that thin port on the bottom of the iPod) is the avenue for trans-ferring both music and information on and off the iPod and for charging the device. Likewise, the USB 2.0 cable included with the iPod can perform double duty. When you string the cable between your iPod and your computer's powered USB 2.0 port, power flows through the cable and charges the iPod's battery. At the same time, this connection allows you to swap data—in the form of music and other files—between the player and the computer.

note The USB cable also can be attached to Apple's optional $29 iPod USB Power Adapter to charge the iPod's battery when it's not connected to a computer.

As the iPod shuffle already comes with a Dock, a USB cable is unnecessary, as is the following item.

iPod Dock Adapter

This adapter looks similar to the Dock cradle adapters included with some iPod accessories. To assist iPod accessory manufacturers, which were forced to come up with a new cradle design every time Apple issued a new iPod, Apple created a single one-size-fits-all-with-the-right-Apple-adapter specification for companies that participate in the Made for iPod program. This is that adapter. Currently, many accessories—including speakers and docks—support this universal adapter.

Dock (iPod shuffle only)

As I mentioned earlier, you power and sync the 2G iPod shuffle through a USB dock bundled in the box. This dock bears a single male headphone jack. Connect the USB side of the cable to a powered USB port to charge and sync the iPod. Jack it into an Apple Power Adapter to charge the iPod.

Guides and documentation

It seems you can't buy something as simple as a toaster these days without also gaining mounds of accompanying documentation. Apple is different in this regard. The current crop of iPods comes with a slim Quick Start guide and a product information pamphlet that carries the fine print.

Given that you own this book, you can skip nearly all the paperwork that comes with your iPod (unless the fine print of licensing agreements helps you sleep at night). At one time, I would have sent you to the bundled CD to gawk at Apple's iPod manual or to install iTunes, but Apple has dispensed with the CD, figuring that you can obtain iTunes and any technical information from Apple's Web site.

Yesterday's iPods

I'd like to think that there are a lot of old iPods being passed from person to person as the original owners trade up. It's quite possible that you have an older iPod yet are new to this whole iPod business. This sidebar is for you. Here's how the various models shake out.

FIRST-GENERATION (1G) IPOD

As the name implies, these are the very first iPod models. Originally released in late 2001 and early 2002, the 1G iPod was offered in 5 and 10 GB configurations, and bore a mechanical scroll wheel—a wheel, unlike the one on later iPods, that actually turned. Nothing on the back of an original 5 GB iPod indicates its storage capacity; the 10 GB model is marked as such on the back plate. These iPods support FireWire connections only and are incompatible with today's Dock-connector accessories. They also don't play files in the Apple Lossless format or record audio from an external source. Like all iPods up to the current full-size iPod, this iPod is incapable of playing video files.

continues on next page

SECOND-GENERATION (2G) IPOD

The second white iPod came in 5, 10, and 20 GB capacities; sported a new, touch-sensitive scroll wheel; included redesigned ear-buds that fit smaller ear canals more comfortably; and slapped a plastic cover over the FireWire port. This iPod bears the same limitations as the 1G iPod in terms of support for Apple Lossless, Dock-connector accessories, audio recording, and video playback.

THIRD-GENERATION (3G) IPOD

Whereas the 2G iPods were an evolutionary release, the 3G play-ers were a redefinition of the original. The new iPods—available in capacities of 10, 15, 20, 30, and 40 GB—were sleeker and lighter. They featured a new front-panel design that placed touch-sen-sitive (and backlit) navigation buttons above the scroll wheel. Gone was the FireWire connector at the top of the iPod, replaced by a proprietary connector at the bottom of the unit that sup-ported both FireWire and USB 2.0 connections. (Charging over USB was not supported on these iPods, however.) A new remote connector was also added to the top of the 3G iPod. This connec-tor was ostensibly for connecting the Apple iPod Remote to the player, but it was later used by other accessories, such as Griffin Technology's iTrip FM transmitter and Belkin's Voice Recorder for iPod.

IPOD MINI (1G AND 2G)

Apple released a smaller version of the iPod in January 2004: the iPod mini. The first generation of minis were available in five col-ors: gold, silver, blue, green, and pink. The original mini was the first iPod to hold a 4 GB hard drive (called a *microdrive*), as well as the first iPod to sport a click wheel. The 2G minis came in brighter shades of blue, green, and pink (gold was discontinued, and the silver model looked the same as the 1G version), and were offered in 4 GB and 6 GB configurations. The mini was discontinued with the introduction of the iPod nano.

continues on next page

FOURTH-GENERATION (4G) IPOD

When Apple announced the 4G iPod in July 2004, it could have done so by proclaiming that the "maxi-mini" was born, for the 4G iPod was, in some ways, closer in design to the iPod mini than to the previous three generations of white iPods. Available in 20 and 40 GB configurations, the 4G iPod bore the same kind of click-wheel controller used on the mini. And like the mini, it could be charged via USB 2.0.

APPLE IPOD + HP, APPLE IPOD MINI + HP, APPLE IPOD SHUFFLE + HP

At one time, Hewlett-Packard sold iPods. No longer. These iPods were unique because ... well, because they were sold by HP. Other than that, they were functionally identical to Apple's iPods. The only real difference between an hPod and an iPod was the warranty that covered the devices. HP's warranty was a bit more generous in terms of when you'd have to begin paying to have your iPod fixed. HP canceled its iPod partnership with Apple in the summer of 2005.

IPOD U2 SPECIAL EDITION (MONOCHROME VERSION)

Though functionally identical to a 20 GB monochrome 4G iPod, this special player was the first "big" iPod to come in colors—specifically, a black face with a red click wheel. Along with a coupon for $50 off U2's entire 400-plus song catalog from Apple's iTunes Store (normally priced at $149), this special iPod also carried the signatures of the four U2 members etched on the back plate.

continues on next page

IPOD PHOTO

You can think of the iPod photo as either a 4G iPod with color and photo capabilities or as the succeeding iPod with color display with *photo* appended to its name. This iPod—available in capacities of 30, 40, and 60 GB—existed as the higher-priced alternative to the monochrome 4G iPod. In addition to putting a bright and colorful face on the now-dull-in-comparison 4G iPod, the iPod photo allowed you to view pictures and slideshows on your iPod (up to 25,000 pictures on the 60 GB model), as well as to project those pictures on an attached television or compatible projector.

IPOD WITH COLOR DISPLAY

Apple did little more than make this iPod's name more cumbersome to differentiate it from the earlier iPod photo; it sported no change worthy of terming it the 5G iPod. With this iPod, all full-size iPods went color. The iPod with color display shipped in 20, 30, and 60 GB configurations.

IPOD SHUFFLE (1G)

The original iPod shuffle was about the size of a pack of gum and could be had in capacities of 512 MB and 1 GB. Unlike the current shuffle, this one bore a male USB connector, which allowed you to jack the iPod into your computer's USB port without the need for a Dock.

IPOD NANO (1G)

This is the original iPod nano. Its face was easily scratched plastic, and its back was shiny silver, like the backs of full-size iPods. It came in capacities of 1, 2, and 4 GB and just two colors (black and white), and it didn't support voice memos.

FIFTH-GENERATION (5G) IPOD

This is the original "iPod with video." It differs from the Late 2006 model in that its screen isn't as bright, and it doesn't offer the current model's alphabetic search feature (more on this in the next chapter).

2

Controls
and Interface

The iPod has rightly been praised for its ease of use. As with all its products, Apple strove to make the iPod as intuitive as possible, placing a limited number of controls and ports on the device and making moving from one screen to another a logical progression. In the following pages, I scrutinize each iPod's controls and examine the screens that populate the display-bearing iPods.

On the Face of It

On the front of your iPod and iPod nano, you'll find a display and set of navigation controls. The shuffle dispenses with the display and provides a simplified set of controls. On the first two generations (1G and 2G) of the iPod, these controls were arrayed around a central scroll wheel and were mechanical—meaning that they moved and activated switches underneath the buttons. On the third-generation (3G) iPods, these controls were placed above the scroll wheel and were touch sensitive; they activated when they came into contact with your flesh but, allegedly, not when a nonfleshy object (such as the walls of your backpack, pocket, or purse) touched them.

Figure 2.1 iPod's click wheel.

The iPod mini, fourth-generation (4G) and later full-size iPods, and the iPod nano bear a click wheel that incorporates the navigation buttons. Unlike the first two generations of the iPod, on which the buttons are arrayed around the outside of the wheel, these buttons are part of the wheel itself (**FIGURE 2.1**). Their sensors sit beneath the wheel at the four compass points, and the scroll wheel sits upon a short spindle that allows it to rock in all directions. To activate one of the buttons, just press the wheel in the direction of that button.

The iPod shuffle's navigation controls are based on this wheel idea but don't duplicate it exactly. The ring around the center button is far narrower than you'll find on the mama and papa iPods, and it functions somewhat differently. Because of the shuffle's lack of a display and different controls, I'll discuss it separately.

The iPod display

Near the top of the standard iPod sits a 2.5-inch-diagonal, color liquid crystal display that can show up to 65,536 colors at a resolution of 320 by 240 pixels. Like the nano, the standard iPod display features backlighting (illumination that makes the display easier to read in dim light), which you can switch on by holding down the Menu button at the top of the click wheel. On all current display-bearing iPods, you can also switch on backlighting by adding the Backlight command to the iPod's main screen and then selecting Backlight on that screen. (To add the command, follow this path from the main screen: Settings > Main Menu, scroll down to Backlight, and press the Center button so that Off turns to On.) iPods older than the fifth-generation (5G) iPod and iPod nano include the Backlight command on the main screen by default.

Measured diagonally, the nano's color display is an inch smaller than that of the standard iPod, yet it projects nearly as much text as its larger sibling (it's missing the Video command on the main screen). It does this by using a different font from the one used on the standard iPod.

iPod and iPod nano controls

The controls of the iPod, iPod mini, and iPod nano have a lot in common—so much that it only makes sense to discuss them together. All feature the six controls described in the following sections.

Play/Pause button

If you scan the surface of your iPod or iPod nano, you'll notice that it bears no recognizable On/Off switch. To switch on current iPods and iPod nanos, press the Center button. On earlier models, start up by using the Play/Pause button. To switch off any display-bearing iPod, press and hold its Play/Pause button for about 3 seconds. This button is located at the bottom of the iPod control wheel on older iPods, in the third position in the row of buttons on 3G iPods, and at the bottom of the click wheel on today's standard iPods and iPod nanos. As you'd expect, pressing this button also starts and pauses music and video playback. On color iPods (including the nano), pressing this button while viewing a photo album initiates a slideshow.

Previous/Rewind button

This button is located on the far-left side of the wheel on 1G, 2G, and click-wheel iPods. It's the far-left button on 3G iPods. In most cases, pressing this button once takes you to the beginning of the currently playing song or video. Movies purchased from the iTunes Store are the exception. If these movies have chapter marks (and all do, as far as I know), pressing Previous moves the movie to the previous chapter. Press Previous multiple times to move back multiple chapters. If you've pressed Previous more times than there are chapters, you're taken back to the Movies screen. Pressing Previous twice in succession in a music playlist moves you to the previous song in the playlist. Do this with a video track, and you're taken back to the Video screen or that video's playlist screen. Hold down Previous to rewind through a song, video, or movie. When you rewind or fast-forward through a song, video, or movie, you move in small increments at first. As you continue to hold the button down, you move in larger increments.

On color iPods, the Previous/Rewind button also moves you back through a slideshow.

Next/Fast Forward button

Look to the far right on 1G, 2G, and click-wheel iPods; look to the rightmost button on 3G iPods. This button behaves similarly to the Previous button. Press it when viewing a movie to move forward through chapters. Press this button once to go to the next song in a music playlist. Press it once while viewing a nonmovie video, and you're returned to the Video screen or that video's playlist screen. Hold Forward down to fast-forward through a song, video, or movie. As is true of rewinding, fast-forwarding moves you through small increments of a song or video at first. As you continue to hold the button down, the increments get larger.

On color iPods (including the nano), the Next/Fast Forward button advances you through a slideshow.

Menu button

Pressing the well-marked Menu button takes you back through the interface the way you came. If you've moved from the main iPod screen to the

Browse screen, for example, and you press the Menu button, you'll move back to the main iPod screen. If you've moved from the main iPod screen through the Playlist screen to a particular song within a particular playlist, each time you press the Menu button, you'll move back one screen.

Holding the Menu button down for about 2 seconds turns backlighting on or off.

Scroll wheel

Inside the ring of buttons on 1G and 2G iPods, below the bevy of buttons on 3G iPods, and marked with the navigation controls on click-wheel iPods is the scroll wheel. Moving your thumb clockwise highlights items below the selected item; moving the wheel counterclockwise highlights items above the selected item. If a window is larger than the display, moving the scroll wheel causes the window to scroll up or down when the first or last item in the list is highlighted.

You also use the scroll wheel to adjust volume and to move to a particular location in a song, video, or movie.

Center button

The bull's-eye of all iPods—the Center button—selects a menu item. If the Settings menu item is selected, for example, pushing the Center button moves you to the Settings screen, where you can select additional settings.

When you press the Center button while a song or video is playing and the Play screen is visible, you move to another Play screen, where you can *scrub* (quickly navigate forward and back with the scroll wheel) your song or video. On 5G iPods, if you press the Center button twice when a video is playing, a brightness control appears. On 3G and 4G monochrome iPods and iPod minis, pressing this button twice while a song plays moves you to a rating screen, where you can assign a rating of one to five stars to the song that's playing (**FIGURE 2.2**).

Figure 2.2
Display-bearing iPods let you rate songs from one to five stars.

On color iPods, you may have to press the Center button a time or two more to get past the Album Artwork screen (and, in the case of the iPod with video and iPod nano, the Lyrics screen) to reach the Ratings screen. You won't find a ratings screen for videos or movies on the 5G iPod.

iPod shuffle status light and controls

There's no need to mention the shuffle's display, because it has none. It does have a status light that tells you what it's doing, however, as well as navigation controls on the front. The 2G model also has power and play-order switches on the bottom, and the 1G shuffle has a single power/play-order switch on the back. Here's how they work.

Status light

The top and bottom of the 2G iPod shuffle include small LEDs. When you first turn on a charged shuffle, a light glows green on these LEDs for about 3 seconds. When you press Play or any part of the outer ring, the green light briefly appears again. If you pause playback, the green light blinks for just under a minute. When you lock the shuffle, an amber status light blinks three times rapidly. Press any of the controls while the shuffle is locked, and you'll see this same amber glow.

When you plug the shuffle into a power source, its amber light will glow continuously and then switch to the green LED when the shuffle is fully charged.

Outer ring

Figure 2.3 iPod shuffle's control wheel.

Photo courtesy of Apple Computer

The ring that surrounds the inner Play/Pause button handles track "navigation" (such as it is) and volume control (**FIGURE 2.3**). Press the top part of the ring (marked with a +) to increase volume. Press the bottom of the ring (marked with a –) to turn the volume down. The right side of the ring controls the iPod's Next/Fast Forward function; press once to move to the next track, or press and hold to fast-forward through the currently playing track.

The Previous/Rewind button on the left side of the ring works like the Previous/Rewind buttons on other iPods. Press once, and the currently playing song starts at the beginning. Press twice quickly in succession to move to the previous song in the playlist.

Play/Pause button

Yes, the Play/Pause button does what it says. With the shuffle switched on, press the button once to play; press it again to pause.

Because the shuffle has so few controls, Apple has pressed this button into service to perform other jobs. To go to the beginning of a playlist, for example, press Play/Pause three times quickly (within a second). To lock the iPod (disable its buttons), press and hold the button for about 3 seconds. To unlock it, press and hold the button again.

note When you lock the shuffle, its status light blinks three times. When you unlock it, the light briefly glows green.

Figure 2.4 iPod shuffle's power and play-order switches.

Photo courtesy of Apple Computer

Power and play-order switches

The top of the shuffle has two switches—one for power and another that toggles between Repeat and Shuffle modes (**FIGURE 2.4**). Push the power switch to the right to turn the shuffle on. Push the play-order switch to the left and the iPod will live up to its name and shuffle its playlist randomly. Push this switch to the right and the shuffle will play its playlist, in order, from beginning to end before repeating.

Battery-status button/light

Unlike the previous iPod shuffle, which carried its own battery status light, the 2G iPod shuffle indicates its current charge through the LEDs found on the top and bottom of the player. To see how much charge you have left, quickly flick the power switch off and then on. The shuffle will continue playing if you do this rapidly enough. A green-glowing LED indicates a full charge (even after the shuffle has played for several hours). If you see an amber light, the shuffle is low on power. A red light indicates that it's really low on power, and no light at all tells you that the shuffle is completely drained and should be plugged into a power source to charge.

Ports and connectors: Dock-connector iPods

The iPod doesn't work by osmosis. You need a hole for the sound to get out (and, in some cases, in), and another hole for moving data on and off the device. Here's what you'll find on the Dock-connector iPods.

Headphone jack and Hold switch

The 3G and all click-wheel iPods except the iPod nano and 5G iPod sport a Headphone jack, a Hold switch, and an iPod Remote Control connector up top (**Figure 2.5** and **Figure 2.6**).

Figure 2.5 Top of the 4G iPod.

Figure 2.6 Port cap atop the iPod mini.

You'll find the iPod nano's Hold switch on top but the Headphone port on the bottom (**FIGURE 2.7**). The nano and 5G iPod have no Remote Control port. The Headphone jack and Hold switch provide audio output and disable the iPod's controls, working nearly the same way on today's iPod and iPod nano as they did on older models.

Figure 2.7
Top of the 2G
iPod nano.

tip I say *nearly* because the Headphone jack, in combination with the Remote Control connector on 3G-and-later standard iPods up to the 5G iPod, supports not only audio output, but also audio input. With a compatible microphone, you can record low-quality audio (8 kHz) on these iPods. The 5G iPod and 2G iPod nano support higher-resolution audio recording via their Dock Connector ports and a compatible microphone. See Chapter 6 for more on compatible iPod microphones.

note The standard color iPod's Headphone jack is different from that on other iPods in that it's capable of also transmitting composite video. Though an iPod nano can display pictures on its screen, it doesn't support connections to external video devices.

Dock Connector port

On the bottom of the Dock-connector iPod, you'll find a proprietary port that handles both power and data chores for the device. This port, on the bottom of the 3G iPods and all click-wheel iPods save the iPod nano and the 5G iPod, supports data transfer via both FireWire and USB 2.0 (**Figure 2.8** and **Figure 2.9**). The nano and 5G iPod can be charged via FireWire but sync only over USB (**Figure 2.10**).

Figure 2.8 Dock Connector port at the bottom of the iPod.

Figure 2.9 iPod mini's Dock Connector port.

Figure 2.10 2G iPod nano's Headphone and Dock Connector ports.

Ports and connectors: iPod shuffle

The iPod shuffle has exactly one hole: the Headphone port (**Figure 2.11**). On the original iPod shuffle, this port was exactly what its name implies: a place to plug in your earbuds or other headphones.

Figure 2.11 2G iPod shuffle's Headphone/ Dock port.

Photo courtesy of Apple Computer

The 2G iPod shuffle's Headphone port serves two purposes. You not only listen to music through this port, but also sync and charge the iPod through it via the shuffle's dock. To charge or sync your shuffle, plug the dock cable into a powered USB 2.0 port on your computer, then slip the shuffle in the dock, so that its Headphone port slides over the dock's minplug.

Figure 2.12
USB connector at the bottom of the 1G iPod shuffle

The original shuffle charges and syncs differently. Flip this shuffle over, pull off its protective cap, and spy the USB connector (**Figure 2.12**). Plug that into your computer's powered USB 2.0 port to charge the iPod and then transfer music and data to it.

Navigating the Screens

Considering how easy the iPod is to use, it's hard to believe the number of navigation screens that make up its interface. In the following pages, I scrutinize each screen. Except where indicated, interfaces for the standard iPod and the iPod nano are identical.

Main screen

The main screen (**Figure 2.13**), which displays the word *iPod* at the top, is your gateway to the iPod. In a way, it's akin to the Mac's Finder or Windows' My Computer window—a place to get started.

Figure 2.13
iPod's main screen.

The 5G iPod's main screen contains these commands:

- Music
- Extras
- Photos
- Settings
- Videos
- Shuffle Songs
- Now Playing (if a song is playing or paused)

Color 4G iPods and the iPod nano include a similar list of commands but without the Videos command.

In the main screen on an iPod mini and an original monochrome iPod running iPod Software 1.3 Updater through iPod Software 3.1.1 Updater (the version of the iPod software current for 4G iPods as this book goes to press), you can, by default, select the following items (**FIGURE 2.14**):

- Music
- Shuffle Songs
- Extras
- Backlight
- Settings
- Now Playing (if a song is playing or paused)

Figure 2.14 iPod mini's screen.

Earlier versions of the iPod software do not include the Backlight command; instead, they offer an About command. On iPods running iPod Software 1.3 Updater or later, the About command is available in the Settings screen (described later in this chapter). Here's what you'll find within each item.

Music

When you choose the Music command and press the Center button, the resulting Music screen reveals these entries: Playlists, Artists, Albums, Songs, Podcasts (click-wheel iPods only), Genres, Composers, Audiobooks, and (on the 5G iPod released in September 2006) Search (**Figure 2.15**). I explain the purpose of all these entries in the following sections.

Figure 2.15
iPod's Music screen.

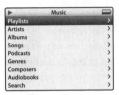

Playlists

Regardless of which iPod you're using, when you choose Playlists and press the Center button, you'll see a screen that contains the playlists you have downloaded to your iPod (**Figure 2.16**).

Figure 2.16
Playlists screen.

These playlists are created and configured in iTunes or another music application, such as the Windows programs Anapod Explorer and XPlay. How you configure them is up to you. You may, for example, want to gather all your jazz favorites in one playlist and put ska in another. Or, if you have an iPod shared by the family, Dad may gather his psychedelic songs of the '60s in his personal playlist, whereas sister Sue creates a playlist full of hip-hop and house music. When I discuss iTunes and other music applications in later chapters, I'll look at additional approaches for putting together playlists.

note You may notice a couple of other playlists that you didn't create: '90s Music, My Top Rated, Recently Added, Recently Played, and Top 25 Most Played, for example. These are Smart Playlists—playlists automatically created by iTunes. As their names hint, these playlists list songs recorded in the '90s, songs that you think are just swell, songs that you've just placed in iTunes, songs you've played in the not-too-distant past, and songs that you've played more often than others.

After you select a playlist and press the Center button, the songs within that playlist appear in a scrollable screen (**Figure 2.17**), and the name of the playlist appears at the top of the screen. Just select the song you want to play, and press the Center button. When you do, you'll move to the Now Playing screen (**Figure 2.18**), which displays the number of songs in the playlist, the name of the song playing, the artist, and the name of the album from which the song came.

Figure 2.17 *(left)* Songs within a playlist.

Figure 2.18 *(right)* Now Playing screen.

On color iPods and iPod nanos, you'll also see a picture of the album cover if the song has this information embedded in it and iTunes' "Display album artwork on your iPod" option is enabled. (Monochrome iPods don't display album artwork.) Also appearing in this screen are two timer displays: elapsed time and remaining time. The screen also contains a graphic thermometer display that gives you a visual representation of how far along you are in the song.

note Text that runs off the screen in the Song, Artist, and Album screens is treated differently on color iPods and the iPod nano than it is on other iPods. Earlier iPods and the iPod mini place an ellipsis (...) at the end of an entry that exceeds the width of the screen. A color-display iPod will scroll selected text from right to left if it's longer than the screen can accommodate.

Two additional screens lie beyond the Now Playing screen, one reached by using the scroll wheel and the other by pressing the Center button. If you turn the scroll wheel, you'll move to a screen nearly identical to the Now Playing screen where you can adjust the iPod's volume (**Figure 2.19**). Turn clockwise, and you'll raise the volume; turn counterclockwise to lower it. If you press the Center button while you're in the Now Playing screen, you'll be able to scrub through the song (**Figure 2.20**).

Figure 2.19 *(left)* Now Playing screen's volume control.

Figure 2.20 *(right)* Now Playing screen's scrub control.

Like the Now Playing screen, the scrub screen carries a thermometer display that indicates the playing location with a small diamond. Just push the scroll wheel back or forth to start scrubbing. Stop moving the scroll wheel in either of these screens, and you'll return to Now Playing after a couple of seconds.

The color iPod and iPod nano include two or three more screens in addition to the scrub screen. On these iPods, if you have album artwork embedded in a track, pressing the Center button twice while in the Now Playing screen shows you a full-screen version of the album cover. If you've added lyrics to a track with iTunes 5 or later, pressing the Center button three times from the Now Playing screen will take you to a Lyrics screen. If you have added lyrics, pressing the Center button four times takes you to a Ratings screen, where you can assign a rating of one to five stars. (If you haven't added lyrics, three clicks takes you to the Ratings screen.)

On-The-Go (Dock-connector iPods)

Scroll to the bottom of the Playlists screen on a Dock-connector iPod, and you'll find an additional playlist that you didn't create: the On-The-Go playlist (**Figure 2.21**).

Figure 2.21
The On-The-Go screen lets you create custom playlists directly on the iPod.

Introduced with iPod Software 2.0 Updater, this play-list is a special one that you create directly on the iPod. It's particularly useful when you need to create a new playlist *right now* and don't have a computer you can plug your iPod into. It works this way:

1. Select a song, artist, playlist, or album.

2. Hold down the Center button until the selected item flashes a few times.

   This flashing indicates that the item has been added to the On-The-Go playlist.

3. Repeat this procedure for any other songs, artists, playlists, and albums you want to add to the list.

4. When you're ready to play your selections, choose On-The-Go from the Playlists screen, and press the Center button.

   In the resulting On-The-Go screen, you'll see a list of songs you've added to the list, in the order in which you added them. (The song, artist, playlist, or album you selected first will appear at the top of the list.)

5. Press the Center button to begin playing the playlist.

To clear the On-The-Go playlist, scroll to the bottom of the playlist, and select Clear Playlist. In the resulting Clear screen, select Clear Playlist; then press the Center button.

When you sync a 3G iPod that's running the iPod Software 2.1 Updater or later, the On-The-Go playlist you created appears in iTunes' Source list as well as in the iPod's Playlist screen—thus ensuring that you don't lose the contents of the playlists you so carefully created on the iPod. Each such playlist is numbered successively: On-The-Go 1, On-The-Go 2, and On-The-Go 3, for example. These playlists are copied back to your iPod, and the On-The-Go entry is cleared.

On the click-wheel iPods running the latest iPod Software Updater, Apple expands the On-The-Go playlist's capabilities, allowing you to create multiple On-The-Go playlists on your iPod. To do so, follow these steps:

1. Follow the steps above to create an On-The-Go playlist.

2. Scroll to the On-The-Go entry in the Playlists screen, and press the Center button.

   The songs you added to your playlists appear in the On-The-Go screen.

3. Scroll to the bottom of the On-The-Go screen, select Save Playlist, and press the Center button.

4. In the resulting Save screen, scroll to Save Playlist, and press the Center button.

   Your playlist will be saved as New Playlist 1. Each time you save a new On-The-Go playlist, it will be called New Playlist and assigned a number one greater than the last New Playlist created.

When you synchronize your click-wheel iPod with iTunes, your saved On-The-Go playlists will appear successively numbered in iTunes, bearing the name

On-The-Go: On-The-Go 1, On-The-Go 2, and (you guessed it) On-The-Go 3, for example. During synchronization, these On-The-Go playlists are copied to your iPod, and the New Playlist entries are removed.

Artists

The Artists screen displays the names of any artists on your iPod (**FIGURE 2.22**). Choose an artist's name and press the Center button, and you'll be transported to that artist's screen, where you have the opportunity to play every song on your iPod by that artist or select a particular album by that artist.

Figure 2.22
Artists screen.

You'll also spy the All entry at the top of the Artists screen. Should you choose this entry, you'll be taken to the All Albums screen, where you can select all albums by all artists. The All Albums screen contains an All command of its own. Select this command, and you'll move to the All Songs screen, which lists all songs by all artists on your iPod. (But if a song doesn't have an artist entry, the song won't appear in this screen.)

Albums

Choose the Albums entry and press the Center button, and you'll see every album on your iPod (**Figure 2.23**). Choose an album and press the Center button to play the album from beginning to end. The Albums screen also contains an All button, which, when selected, displays all the songs on all the albums on your iPod. (If the song doesn't have an album entry, it won't appear in this screen.)

Figure 2.23
Albums screen.

> **note**
>
> An album entry can contain a single song. As long as the album field has been filled in for a particular song within iTunes or another iPod-compatible application (I'll discuss this topic in Chapter 3), that song will appear in the Albums screen.

Songs

Choose Songs and press the Center button, and you'll see a list of all the songs on your iPod (**Figure 2.24**).

Figure 2.24
Songs screen.

Podcasts (click-wheel iPods only)

As you'll learn later in the book, *podcasts* are Internet broadcasts that you download and place on your iPod for later listening. Podcasts downloaded through the iTunes Store are routed to your iPod and placed under this entry on click-wheel iPods (**Figure 2.25**). On earlier iPods, you'll find the Podcasts entry in the Playlists screen.

Figure 2.25
Podcasts screen.

Genres

The iPod has the capability to sort songs by genre: Acoustic, Blues, Reggae, and Techno, for example. If a song has been tagged with a genre entry, you can choose it by genre in the Genres screen (**Figure 2.26**).

Composers

The iPod can also group songs by composers. This feature, added in iPod Software 1.2 Updater, allows you to sort classical music more easily (**Figure 2.27**).

Figure 2.26
(left) Genres screen.

Figure 2.27
(right) Composers screen.

Audiobooks

The iPod is capable of playing audiobook files purchased from Audible.com and the iTunes Store. These audiobooks can be identified by their extension: .aa for books bought from Audible.com or .m4b for those bought from the iTunes Store. When an iPod stores one of these specially formatted files, the audiobook's name appears in the iPod's Audiobooks screen (which appears when you choose Audiobooks command in the Music screen and press the Center button).

Search (Late 2006 5G iPod and 2G iPod nano only)

When Apple released the updated 5G iPod and 2G iPod nano in late 2006, it gave them a new Search feature. Select Search and press the Center button, and you'll see a Search screen. Using the scroll wheel, you scroll through an alphanumeric list. When you reach the letter you seek, press the Center button to enter that letter into the Search field. When you do this, a list of matching items appears in the top part of the screen (**Figure 2.28**).

Figure 2.28
Search screen.

Continue scrolling and clicking to enter more letters and numbers to narrow your search. To remove an unwanted character, press the Previous button to erase the last character you entered. When you've entered as many letters as you care to, select Done and press the Center button. Doing so takes you to the Search Results screen, where you'll see a list of all albums, artists, and songs that contain the letter sequence you entered. (Search doesn't work for videos or movies.) Scroll to the item you want and press the Center button to select it.

If you select a song, it will start playing. If you select an album or artist, you'll see an Albums or Artists screen, and you can continue selecting items and pressing the Center button until you get exactly the track you want.

note **The Search feature is smarter than you may think. Although the list of results generally begins with the first letter you've entered, that list can also contain entries that contain the letters you've entered within the body of the item. Entering DC, for example, produces not only AC/DC as an artist entry but also selections that contain the word podcast.**

All 5G iPods (with the latest iPod software) and the 2G iPod nano support one other kind of searching. Navigate to the Artists, Albums, Songs, or Composers screen, and start scrolling. In short order, a square gray overlay will appear in the middle of the screen, including the letter that reflects where you are in the list. If you're scrolling through the Jack Johnson, Jackie Gleason, Jackie Wilson, James Brown, Janis Joplin, and Jayhawks section of your Artists screen, you'll see the letter J overlaid as you scroll.

Photos (color-display iPods only)

The Photo command appears only on iPods with color displays (**FIGURE 2.29**). This command is your avenue for configuring how slideshows are displayed on the iPod and, if you have a full-size color iPod, on an attached television or projector.

Figure 2.29
Photos screen.

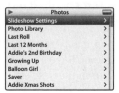

Within the Photos screen, you'll find the following entries (except where noted); below them, you'll see a list of the names of any custom photo albums you imported using iTunes.

Slideshow Settings

The Slideshow Settings screen contains a host of commands, described in the following sections.

Time Per Slide You can configure the iPod so that slideshows are under manual command and you need to press the Next or Previous button to navigate the slideshow. You can also have the iPod change slides automatically every 2, 3, 5, 10, or 20 seconds.

Music Your slideshow can be accompanied by music. From the Slideshow Music screen, choose From iPhoto, Now Playing, Off, one of the playlists on the iPod, or the On-The-Go playlist.

Repeat If you like, you can have your slideshow repeat forever (or at least until the iPod runs out of power). This is a simple On or Off command.

Shuffle Photos This is another On or Off command. Off means that your slides play in order; choose On, and they're displayed randomly.

Transitions The color iPods offer built-in *transitions* (effects that occur when you move from one slide to another). The included effects on the iPod nano are Random (a random mix of effects), Push Across, Push Down, Wipe Across, Wipe Down, and Wipe from Center. The 5G iPod adds Cube Across, Cube Down, Dissolve, Page Flip, Radial, and Swirl.

TV Out (full-size color iPods only) This tells the iPod whether to output its video signal via the Headphone jack or the S-Video port on an attached color iPod's Dock. Off means no signal. Ask means that when you call up a photo library on the iPod and press Play to begin the show, a screen will appear, asking you whether you'd like the TV signal turned on or left off. On means that the iPod will automatically send the signal out the Headphone jack.

tip Turning on TV output depletes the battery charge in a big way. Switch this option on only if you really need it.

TV Signal (full-size color iPods only) The world has two major television standards: NTSC (United States and Japan) and PAL (Europe and Australia). You can choose either for your iPod's video output.

Photo Import (full-size color iPods only) Full-size color iPods can import photos from many digital

cameras using Apple's $29 iPod Camera Connector.
When you connect a supported camera to your
iPod using this device, the Photo Import command
appears in the Photos screen. Click it, and you'll find a
list of all the rolls (import sessions) for photos you've
brought into the iPod.

Photo Library

Press this entry to view all the photos stored on your
iPod. Below the Photo Library entry, you'll find a list of
all the photo albums that iTunes has imported onto
your iPod. Select the album you want to view, and
press Play to view the slideshow.

Videos (5G iPods only)

Not surprisingly, the Videos command is found only
on iPods capable of playing video—which, as this
book goes to press, are both iterations of the 5G iPod.
Within the Videos screen, you'll find this list
of entries.

Video Playlists

As I'll explain in the next chapter, you can create
playlists that contain videos and then copy these
playlists (and their contents) to a compatible iPod.
When you do, those playlists appear when you select
Video Playlists in the Videos screen and press the
Center button. Select a playlist and press the button
again, and you'll see a list of the videos contained in
that playlist. Select an item in the playlist and press
the Center button or Play, and the selected video
will play.

Movies

Within iTunes, you can tag a video as a Movie, Music Video, or TV Show (I'll tell you how in Chapter 3). Any videos that have the Movie tag assigned to them will appear in the list that appears when you select Movies in the Videos screen and press the Center button.

Music Videos

This works the same way as movies. Tag a video as a Music Video in iTunes, and it appears in the Music Videos list.

TV Shows

At the risk of repeating myself, this also works the same way as movies. If you have programs tagged as TV Shows, they appear in this list.

Video Podcasts

The Video Podcasts entry can be a little confusing. There's no way to label videos as video podcasts in iTunes; that must be done by the creators of the video podcasts, in league with the iTunes Store. If you've downloaded a video podcast, and you've set the iPod's preferences correctly within iTunes (I'll show you how in that legendary Chapter 3), your video podcasts should appear in this screen.

Video Settings

Select this command in the Videos screen and press the Center button, and you'll see three options: TV Out, TV Signal, and Widescreen.

TV Out and TV Signal work just as they do in the Slideshow Settings screen. TV Out determines whether your iPod will play its videos on a connected TV or projector, and TV Signal allows you to choose between NTSC and PAL.

Widescreen offers On or Off. Select On to view widescreen movies in their native letterbox format. Choose Off, and the iPod will scale the picture (and chop off either end) so that it fills the iPod's screen or the screen of the TV it's attached to.

Extras

The Extras screen is the means to all the iPod's nonmusical functions—its contacts, calendars, clock, and games. Here's what you'll find for each entry.

Clock

Yes, the iPod can tell time. Clicking Clock displays the current time and date on all iPods. On 3G iPods and all click-wheel iPods except the 5G iPod and nano, clicking Clock also displays commands for setting the iPod's alarm clock, the sleep timer, and the date and time.

The 5G iPod and nano offer a different Clock screen— one that displays both an analog and digital clock in the top part of the screen and a New Clock entry at the bottom of the screen (**FIGURE 2.30**). Select New

Clock and press the Center button to view the Region screen, where you view such regions as Africa, Asia, Europe, and North America. Select a region and press the button again, and choose a city in the resulting City screen.

Figure 2.30
Clock screen.

When you select a clock on one of these iPods and press the Center button, you'll see these settings for that clock: Alarm Clock, Change City, Daylight Saving Time, Delete This Clock, and Sleep Timer.

Alarm Clock

The Alarm Clock screen provides options for turning the alarm on and off, setting the time for the alarm to go off, and specifying the sound the alarm will play (a simple beep or the contents of one of the playlists on your iPod). This function is not available on 1G and 2G iPods.

tip

If the iPod's alarm clock goes off while you're listening to music with headphones, you're likely to miss the alarm if it's set to beep. Unlike alarms tied to calendar events, the alarm clock issues no visual display; it beeps or plays a playlist—that's it. If you think you'll be listening to music when the alarm is configured to perform its lowly job, choose a playlist as an alarm rather than a beep. When the iPod suddenly changes playlists, you'll know that the alarm has gone off.

Change City (5G iPod and nano only)

Click this entry to be taken to the Region screen, where you can choose a new region and city for the clock.

Daylight Saving Time

This is a simple on/off command.

Delete This Clock (5G iPod and nano only)

You know ...

Sleep Timer

To save battery power, the iPod includes a sleep function that powers down your iPod after a certain amount of time has elapsed. The Sleep Timer settings allow you to determine how long an interval of inactivity has to pass before your iPod takes a snooze. The available settings are Off, 15 Minutes, 30 Minutes, 60 Minutes, 90 Minutes, and 120 Minutes. On older iPods, this command is in the Settings screen.

Games

Once upon a time, the iPod had a single hidden game that you could access only if you held down the Center button for several seconds in a particular screen. Apple later decided to reveal this secret game—a form of the classic Breakout game called Brick (**Figure 2.31**)—by placing the Game command in the Extras screen.

Figure 2.31 Brick game screen.

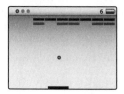

Apple includes three additional games—Music Quiz, Parachute, and Solitaire—with 3G iPods and click-wheel iPods. When you choose the Games option in the Extras screen of these iPods, you'll see listings for Brick, Music Quiz, Parachute, and Solitaire. You can also purchase games created specifically for the 5G iPod from the iTunes Store. When you do and transfer them to your iPod, they'll also appear in the Games screen. I'll discuss these games in the chapter devoted to the store.

To play Brick, just select it and press the Center button. Press the button again to begin the game, and use the scroll wheel to move the paddle.

Music Quiz plays a random portion of a song stored on your iPod, and displays five titles on the iPod's screen (**FIGURE 2.32**).

Figure 2.32 A Music Quiz screen.

Your job is to scroll to the correct title and push the Center button as quickly as your fingers allow. The more swiftly you identify the song, the more points you earn. At the 7-second mark, one of the titles disappears; at 5 seconds, another vanishes; and so on until just one title remains and your time expires.

In Parachute, your job is to rotate the cannon (using the scroll wheel) and blast helicopters and parachutists out of the sky. You lose the game when a certain number of parachutists lands safely or one of them lands directly on your cannon emplacement.

Solitaire is an implementation of the classic Klondike card game (**Figure 2.33**). To play, arrange alternating colors (or lighter and darker suits on non-color iPods) of cards in descending sequence—a sequence that could run jack of hearts, 10 of spades, 9 of diamonds, 8 of clubs, and so on—in the bottom portion of the screen. In the top portion of the window, you arrange cards in an ascending sequence of the same suit— ace, 2, 3, 4, and 5 of hearts, for example.

Figure 2.33
Yes, those little figures represent numbers and suits.

Navigating this game is not completely intuitive. Use the scroll wheel to move the hand pointer to the card you want to move. Press the Center button to move the selected card to the bottom of the screen. Then move the pointer to where you want to place the card, and press Center again. The game tries to be helpful by moving the pointer to the place where you're most likely to place the card.

The Games entry is the last option in the Extras screen on iPods older than the iPod nano and 5G iPod.

Contacts

I'll discuss how to create contacts elsewhere in the book. In the meantime, you need to know only that to access your contacts, you choose Contacts in the Extras screen and press the Center button (**FIGURE 2.34**). Scroll through your list of contacts and press the button again to view the information within a contact. If a contact contains more information than will fit in the display, use the scroll wheel to scroll down the window.

Figure 2.34
Contacts screen.

If you haven't placed any contacts on your iPod, clicking the Contacts command will reveal two entries in the Contacts screen: Instructions and Sample. You can probably guess that selecting Instructions provides you directions on how to move contacts to your iPod. The Sample command shows you what a complete contact looks like.

Calendar

I'll also address calendar creation later in the book, so for now, just know that when you click the Calendar entry on a 3G iPod or click-wheel iPod, you'll see options for viewing all your calendars in a single calendar window; viewing separate calendars (your work or home calendar, for example) if you've created your calendars on the Mac with Apple's iCal; viewing calendars you've created with applications other than iCal under an "Other" heading; viewing To Do items; and setting an alarm for calendar events.

When you select a calendar, the current month is displayed in a window with the current day high-lighted (**FIGURE 2.35**). If a day has an event attached to it, that day displays a small red flag on the 5G iPod and the iPod nano. (Earlier iPods display events as small black rectangles.) Use the scroll wheel to move to a different day; scroll forward to look into the future; and scroll back to be transported back in time. To jump to the next or previous month, use the Next or Previous button, respectively. When you want to see the details of an event, scroll to its day and press the Center button. The details of that day's events will be displayed in the resulting screen.

Figure 2.35
Calendar screen.

The Calendars screen's Alarms command offers three options: Off (no alarm is issued); Beep (a little tinkling sound erupts from the iPod—the iPod itself; not the headphones—and an alarm screen that describes the event is displayed); and Silent (the alarm screen appears without audio accompaniment).

Notes

New with the 3G iPods was a Notes feature that allows you to store text files (up to 4 KB, or about 4,096 characters) on your iPod. To add notes to your iPod, mount the iPod on your computer (the iPod must be configured to appear on the desktop), double-click the iPod to reveal its contents, and drag a text file into the iPod's Notes folder. When you unmount your iPod, you'll find the name of your text file in the Notes area of the Extras screen. The 1G and 2G iPods don't have this function.

Stopwatch (5G iPod and nano only)

The Stopwatch will track total time and lap time. Choose Stopwatch and click the Center button to be taken to the Stopwatch screen, where you select Timer and press Center to access the stopwatch (**Figure 2.36**). The 5G iPod tracks elapsed time as well as Lap time. When you select Start with the scroll wheel and press Center, the watch starts. Spin the wheel to select Lap and press the Center button, and a new lap entry appears below the first.

Figure 2.36 Stopwatch screen.

The iPod nano works similarly; it doesn't list laps on this screen, but it logs one each time you click the Center button when the Lap button is highlighted.

You can add as many as 199 laps to these iPods (and yes, I did click the Center button that many times to find out). When you click Done to stop the watch, it saves your times in a Stopwatch screen. Select one of these entries and click the Center button, and you'll see a summary that displays the date and time of the event; total time; time for each lap; and such summary statistics as total time, longest and shortest laps, and average lap time.

Nike + iPod (iPod nano only)

This command will appear only if you've plugged the Nike + Sport Kit receiver into your iPod nano's Dock Connector port. It leads to a Workout screen that allows you to choose among four main options: Basic, Time, Distance, and Calories. Within a Settings screen, you'll also find menu options for PowerSong (one track you've chosen that will activate with the press of the Center button at a key point of your workout); Spoken Feedback (choose either a male or a female voice to issue feedback); Distances (miles or kilometers); and Sensor, where you calibrate the Sport Kit for your body.

Screen Lock (5G iPod and nano only)

Screen Lock is a feature for . . . well, locking your iPod's screen. Like a cheap bike lock, this lock lets you create a four-digit password using numbers from 0 through 9. The interface features a round combination wheel with four digits above it. To move from one digit to another, use the Next and Previous buttons. Pressing the Center button also takes you to the next digit and, when you reach the final digit, sets the code. When the nano is locked, you can pause and play it, but nothing more; you can't adjust the volume, because turning the wheel adjusts the selected digit. Even when you reset the iPod, it boots back into the Screen Lock screen.

Voice Memos (3G, 4G, full-size color iPods, and 2G iPod nano only)

Late-model standard iPods and the 2G iPod nano can record voice memos with a compatible microphone adapter. When you plug such an adapter into the Headphone jack and Remote Control port, the Voice Memos command appears in the iPod's Extras screen. Currently, only three devices—Belkin's TuneTalk, Griffin Technology's iTalk Pro, and XtremeMac's MicroMemo—are compatible with the latest iPod's voice-recording function.

Click the Center button, and you're taken to the Voice Memos screen, where you can choose to record a new voice memo or play back memos you've already recorded (**FIGURE 2.37**).

Figure 2.37
Voice Memos
screen.

Settings

The Settings screen (**Figure 2.38**) is the path to your iPod preferences—including backlight timer and startup-volume settings, EQ selection, and the language the iPod displays. The following sections look at these settings individually.

Figure 2.38
Settings screen.

About

The About screen is where you'll find the name of your iPod (changeable within iTunes and such Windows players as XPlay), the number of songs (and videos and photos, where applicable) the iPod currently holds, the total hard-drive space and amount of available space, the software version, your iPod's serial number, and the model number. If you have an iPod formatted for Windows, you'll also see the Format Windows entry. (The Mac version of the iPod doesn't bother to tell you that it's formatted for the Macintosh.)

Main Menu

The Main Menu command offers you a way to customize what you see in the iPod's main screen. Choose Main Menu, and press the Center button.

In the resulting screen, you can choose to view a host of commands. To enable or disable a command, press the Center button to toggle the command on or off. To return the main menu to its default setting, choose the Reset Main Menu command, press the Center button, choose Reset in the Reset Menus screen, and press the button again.

Shuffle

Selecting Shuffle and pressing the Center button rotates you through three settings: Off, Songs, and Albums. On iPods without a click wheel, when Shuffle is set to Off, the iPod plays the songs in a playlist in the order in which they appear onscreen. The Songs setting plays all the songs within a selected playlist or album in random order. If no album or playlist is selected, the iPod plays all the songs on the iPod in random order. And the Albums setting plays the songs within each album in order but shuffles the order in which the albums are played.

Repeat

The Repeat setting also offers three options: Off, One, and All. When you choose Off, the iPod won't repeat songs. Choose One, and you'll hear the selected song play repeatedly. Choose All, and all the songs within the selected playlist or album will repeat when the playlist or album has played all the way through. If you haven't selected a playlist or album, all the songs on the iPod will repeat after they've played through.

Volume Limit (5G iPod, nano, and shuffle only)

This feature was added in the middle of 2006 at the request of parents who were afraid their kids would blow out their ears by playing music at too high a volume. On display-bearing iPods, select Volume Limit and press the Center button, and you're taken to a screen where you can adjust the iPod's maximum volume up or down, using the scroll wheel and a typical iPod thermometer display. Press the Center button again, and you see a screen that offers you the option to set a combination for the volume limit—essentially letting you lock your kid's iPod volume to what you consider a safe and sane level.

To limit maximum volume on the iPod shuffle, connect it to your computer, select the shuffle in iTunes' Source list, and in the Settings tab enable the Limit Maximum Volume option. Drag the slider to the desired maximum volume. To demand a password, click the lock icon, and enter and verify a password in the resulting Volume Limit Password dialog box.

Backlight Timer

The iPod's backlight pulls its power from the battery, and when it's left on for very long, it significantly shortens the time you can play your iPod on a single charge. For this reason, Apple includes a timer that automatically switches off backlighting after a certain user-configurable interval. You set that interval by choosing the Backlight Timer setting.

On iPods before the color iPods, the settings available to you are Off, 2 Seconds, 5 Seconds, 10 Seconds,

20 Seconds, and (for those who give not a whit about battery life or who are running the iPod from the Apple Power Adapter) Always On. Color iPods include one additional setting: 15 Seconds.

Brightness (5G iPods only)

With the latest iPod software installed, all 5G iPods include a Brightness command in the Settings menu. Select it, and you can dial your iPod's brightness up or down.

Audiobooks (click-wheel iPods only)

One of the unique features of the click-wheel iPods is their ability to slow down or speed up the playback of audiobooks without changing the pitch of the narrator. When you select Audiobooks in the Settings screen, you're offered three options in the resulting Audiobooks screen: Slower, Normal, and Faster. The Slower and Faster commands slow or speed playback by about 25 percent, respectively.

You're likely thinking that it would take a minor miracle to pull this off without making the book sound odd. You're right; it would. And so far, Apple has failed to achieve this miracle. When you slow down an audiobook, the resulting audio sounds like it was recorded in a particularly reverberant bathroom; you hear a very short echo after each word. Files that are speeded up appear to have lost all the spaces between words, making the book sound as though it's being read by an overcaffeinated auctioneer.

EQ

EQ (or *equalization*) is the process of boosting or cutting certain frequencies in the audio spectrum—making the low frequencies louder and the high frequencies quieter, for example. If you've ever adjusted the bass and treble controls on your home or car stereo, you get the idea.

The iPod comes with the same EQ settings as iTunes. Those settings include

- Off
- Bass Booster
- Classical
- Deep
- Flat
- Jazz
- Loudness
- Piano
- R & B
- Small Speakers
- Treble Booster
- Vocal Booster

- Acoustic
- Bass Reducer
- Dance
- Electronic
- Hip Hop
- Latin
- Lounge
- Pop
- Rock
- Spoken Word
- Treble Reducer

Although you can listen to each EQ setting to get an idea of what it does, you may find it easier to open iTunes; choose View > Show Equalizer; and in the resulting Equalizer window, choose the various EQ settings from the window's pop-up menu. The equalizer's 10-band sliders will show you which frequencies have been boosted and which have been cut. Any slider that appears above the 0 dB line indicates a frequency that has been boosted. Conversely, sliders that appear below 0 dB have been cut.

Compilations (color iPods only)

Songs are usually given the compilations tag if they're part of a greatest-hits package or soundtrack album. Color iPods include a Compilations entry that lists all the albums with the Compilations tag. You can switch this on or off. When it's switched on, a Compilations entry appears in the Music screen.

Sound Check

Sound Check attempts to maintain a consistent volume among all the songs on your iPod. Before Sound Check arrived on the scene, you'd constantly fiddle with the iPod's volume because one song was too loud, the next too quiet, the next quieter still, and the next painfully loud. Sound Check does its best to produce volumes that don't vary so wildly.

To use Sound Check, you must first enable the Sound Check option in the Playback pane of iTunes' Preferences window. iTunes will adjust the volume settings of the tracks in its Library, and when those tracks are transferred to your iPod, they will maintain the Sound Check settings imposed by iTunes.

note Sound Check won't balance volumes on a per-album basis. This is a problem, because audio engineers intentionally make some songs softer than others—ballads, for example. Sound Check ruins this loud/soft album-track relationship.

Contrast (not available on color iPods)

To change the display's contrast, select the Contrast setting, press the Center button, and use the scroll wheel to darken or lighten the display.

Color iPods don't include any controls for changing the brightness, contrast, or color balance of the screen.

Clicker

This option makes your iPod's click-wheel actually click—a handy option when you're scrolling through your iPod without looking at it. It provides audible feedback when, for example, you're trying to move to the next command or playlist while driving. When you choose Clicker on a click-wheel iPod other than the 5G iPod and press the Center button, you have four options: Off, Speaker, Headphones, and Both. As the names imply, Speaker causes the iPod to emit an audible click sound from a tiny built-in speaker; Headphones plays the clicks through the Headphone jack; and Both channels the click sound through both speakers and the Headphone jack.

The 5G iPod and iPods before the click-wheel models allow you only to turn the clicker on and off. Those non–click wheelers produce no click through the headphones. The 5G iPod either sounds the click through both the headphones and internally or not at all.

Date & Time

The Date & Time command is your means of setting the time zone that your iPod inhabits, as well as the current date and time. On 3G iPods and all click-wheel iPods except the 5G iPod and iPod nano, this command is also accessible from the Date & Time command in the Clock screen.

Set Time Zone Click this command, and in the resulting Time Zone screen, choose your time zone—anything between and including Eniwetok to Auckland. This function is not available on 1G and 2G iPods.

Set Time & Date Select and click this command to set the iPod's date and time. Use the scroll wheel to change the hour, minutes, AM/PM, date, month, and year values, and use the Forward and Previous buttons to move from value to value. This function is not available on 1G and 2G iPods.

Time Use this command to display a 12- or 24-hour clock. This function is not available on 1G and 2G iPods.

Time in Title This command allows the iPod to display the time in the iPod's title bar. This function is not available on 1G and 2G iPods.

tip On 3G-and-later iPods, the Set Time Zone, Set Date & Time, Time, and Time in Title commands are also available in the Date & Time screen that's accessible from the Settings screen.

Contacts

The Contacts setting allows you to sort your contacts by last or first name and to display those contacts by last or first name.

Language

All iPods except the 5G iPod and nano can display 14 languages: English, Japanese, French, German, Spanish, Italian, Danish, Dutch, Norwegian, Swedish, Finnish, Korean, and Chinese (Traditional and Simplified). The 5G iPod and nano display seven additional languages.

Legal

If you care to view a few copyright notices, feel free to choose the Legal setting and press the Center button.

Reset All Settings

As the name implies, selecting Reset All Settings, pressing the Center button, and selecting Reset returns the iPod to its default settings. Your iPod's music will stay right where it is; this command just restores the interface to the way it was when the iPod came out of the box.

Shuffle Songs

One might think that choosing this option causes the iPod to play all the material on the iPod in random order. Not exactly. Shuffle Songs changes its behavior based on the Shuffle setting in the iPod's Settings screen. It works this way:

If you press Shuffle Songs when Shuffle is set to Off or to Songs, the iPod will play songs at random. (Note that it won't play any files it recognizes as audiobooks.)

If you press Shuffle Songs when Shuffle is set to Albums, the iPod picks an album at random and then plays the songs on that album in succession (the order in which they appear on the album). When that album finishes playing, the iPod plays a different album.

Note that if you also switch the Repeat command in the Settings menu to All and press Shuffle Songs, the iPod plays through all the songs on the iPod in the order determined by the Shuffle command and then repeats them in the same order in which they were shuffled originally. If you have three songs on your iPod—A, B, and C—and the iPod shuffles them to be in B, C, A order, when they repeat, they'll repeat as B, C, and A. The iPod won't reshuffle them.

EQ and the iPod

Apple was kind enough to include a configurable equalizer (EQ) as part of the iPod Software 1.1 Updater and later, but the way that the EQ settings in iTunes and the iPod interact is a little confusing. Allow me to end that confusion.

In iTunes, you can assign an EQ setting to songs individually by clicking the song, pressing Command-I (Mac) or Ctrl+I (Windows), clicking the Options tab, and then choosing an EQ setting from the Equalizer Preset menu. When you move songs to your iPod, these EQ settings move right along with them, but you won't be able to use them unless you configure the iPod correctly.

If, for example, you have EQ switched off on the iPod, songs that have assigned EQ presets won't play with those settings. Instead, your songs will play without the benefit of EQ. If you set the iPod's EQ to Flat, the EQ setting that you preset in iTunes will play on the iPod. If you select one of the other EQ settings on the iPod (Latin or Electronic, for example), songs without EQ presets assigned in iTunes will use the iPod EQ setting. Songs with EQ settings assigned in iTunes will use the iTunes setting.

If you'd like to hear how a particular song sounds on your iPod with a different EQ setting, start playing the song on the iPod, press the Menu button until you return to the Main screen, select Settings, select EQ, and then select one of the EQ settings. The song will immediately take on the EQ setting you've chosen, but this setting won't stick on subsequent playback. If you want to change the song's EQ permanently, you must do so in iTunes.

3

iTunes and You

A high-performance automobile is little more than an interesting amalgam of metal and plastic if it's missing tires and fuel. Sure, given the proper slope (and, perhaps, a helpful tailwind), that car is capable of movement, but the resulting journey leaves much to be desired. So, too, the iPod is a less-capable music-making vehicle without Apple's multitrick media manager/player, iTunes. The two—like coffee and cream, dill and pickle, and Fred and Ginger—were simply meant for each other.

To best understand what makes the iPod's world turn, you must be familiar with how it and iTunes 7 work together to move music (and pictures and videos, in the case of some recent iPods) on and off your iPod. In the following pages, you'll learn just that.

Rip a CD

Apple intended the process of converting audio-CD music to computer data to be painless, and it is. Here's how to go about it:

1. Launch iTunes.

2. Insert an audio CD into your computer's CD or DVD drive.

   By default, iTunes will try to identify the CD you've inserted and log on to the Web to download the CD's track information—a very handy feature for those who find typing such minutia to be tedious. The CD appears in iTunes' Source list under the Devices heading, and the track info appears in the Song list to the right (**FIGURE 3.1**).

Figure 3.1 This album's song tracks were downloaded from the Web automatically by iTunes.

3. iTunes then throws up a dialog box asking whether you'd like to import the tracks from the album into your iTunes library; click Yes and it does, or click No and it doesn't.

   You can change this behavior in the Importing tab within the Advanced iTunes Preferences window. There, you find an On CD Insert pop-up menu. With the options in that menu, you can direct iTunes to show the CD, begin playing it, ask to import it (the default), import it, or import it and then eject it.

Figure 3.2
iTunes' Import CD button: Let 'er rip.

4. If you decided earlier not to import the audio but now would like to, simply select the CD in the Source list and click the Import CD button in the bottom-right corner of the iTunes window (**Figure 3.2**).

To import only certain songs, uncheck the boxes next to the songs you don't want to import. Click the Import CD button to import just those songs that have a check mark next to them.

iTunes begins encoding the files via the method chosen in the Importing tab of the Advanced pane of the iTunes Preferences window (**Figure 3.3**). By default, iTunes imports songs in AAC format at 128 Kbps.

Figure 3.3 The Importing panel of Tunes' Advanced iPod preferences pane.

5. Click on Music in the Library section of the iTunes Source list.

You'll find the songs you just imported somewhere in the song list.

6. To listen to a song, click its name in the list and then click the Play button or press the spacebar.

Import Business: File Formats and Bit Rates

MP3, MPEG-4, AAC, AIFF, WAV . . . is the computer industry incapable of speaking plain English!?

It may seem so, given the plethora of acronyms floating through modern-day Technotopia. But the lingo and the basics behind it aren't terribly difficult to understand.

MP3, AAC, AIFF, and WAV are audio file formats. The compression methods used to create MP3 and AAC files are termed *lossy* because the encoder removes information from the original sound file to create these smaller files. Fortunately, these encoders are designed to remove the information you're least likely to miss—audio frequencies that you can't hear easily, for example.

AIFF and WAV files are uncompressed, containing all the data from the original. When a Macintosh pulls audio from an audio CD, it does so in AIFF format, which is the native uncompressed audio format used by Apple's QuickTime technology. WAV is a variant of AIFF and is used extensively with the Windows operating system.

continues on next page

iTunes supports one other compression format: Apple Lossless. This is termed a lossless encoder because the encoder doesn't shrink the file by removing portions of the audio spectrum; rather, it removes redundant data. This scheme allows you to retain all the audio quality of the original file while producing a copy just over half the size of that original file.

iTunes and the 5G iPod also support the H.264 and MPEG-4 video formats. These too are compressed formats that allow you to fit a great big movie on a tiny little iPod.

Now that you're familiar with these file formats, let's touch on resolution as it applies to audio files.

You probably know that the more pixels per inch a digital photograph has, the crisper the image (and the larger the file). Resolution applies to audio as well. But audio defines resolution by the number of kilobytes per second (Kbps) contained in an audio file. *With files encoded similarly*, the higher the kilobyte count, the better-sounding the file (and the larger the file).

I emphasize "with files encoded similarly" because the quality of the file depends a great deal on the encoder used to compress it. Many people claim that if you encode a file at 128 Kbps in both the MP3 and AAC formats, the AAC file will sound better.

The Import Using pop-up menu lets you choose to import files in AAC, AIFF, Apple Lossless, MP3, or WAV format. All display-bearing iPods can play files encoded in the AAC, MP3, AIFF, and WAV formats. Only Dock-connector iPods can play songs formatted with the Apple Lossless Encoder. The 2G iPod shuffle can play all these formats except Apple Lossless. The original shuffle can't play AIFF or Apple Lossless files.

continues on next page

The Setting pop-up menu is where you choose the resolution of the AAC and MP3 files encoded by iTunes. iTunes' default setting is High Quality (128 Kbps). To change this setting, choose Custom from the Setting pop-up and, in the resulting AAC Encoder window, choose a different setting—in a range from 16 to 320 Kbps—from the Stereo Bit Rate pop-up menu (**FIGURE 3.4**). Files encoded at a high bit rate sound better than those encoded at a low bit rate (such as 96 Kbps). But files encoded at higher bit rates also take up more space on your hard drive and iPod.

Figure 3.4
AAC encoding options.

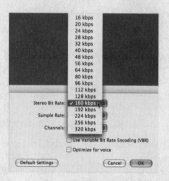

The bit rate options for MP3 importing include Good Quality (128 Kbps), High Quality (160 Kbps), and Higher Quality (192 Kbps). If you don't care for these settings, choose Custom from this same pop-up menu. In the MP3 Encoder dialog box that appears, you can choose a bit rate ranging from 8 Kbps to 320 Kbps.

Resolution is important for video as well. The greater the bit rate of a movie, music video, or TV show, the better-looking the resulting video will be. Fortunately, for the purposes of this slim volume, iTunes doesn't require that you muck with encoding video in any way, shape, or form. Either the movie is encoded in another application in such a way that it plays on your iPod, or it isn't. I'll reveal the secrets of encoding video for the iPod in Chapter 7.

Move Music into iTunes

Ripping CDs isn't the only way to put music files on your computer. Suppose that you've downloaded some audio files from the Web and want to put them in iTunes. You have three ways to do that:

- In iTunes, choose File > Add to Library.

  When you choose this command, the Add to Library window appears. Navigate to the file, folder, or volume you want to add to iTunes, and click Choose (**FIGURE 3.5**). iTunes decides which files it thinks it can play and adds them to the Library.

Figure 3.5 The Add to Library navigation window.

- Drag files, folders, or entire volumes to the iTunes icon in Mac OS X's Dock; the iTunes icon in Windows' Start menu (if you've pinned iTunes to this menu); or the iTunes icon in either operating system (at which point iTunes launches and adds the dragged files to the Library).

- Drag files, folders, or entire volumes into iTunes' main window or the Library entry in the Source list.

  In the Mac versions of iTunes, by default you'll find songs in the iTunes Music folder within the iTunes folder inside the Music folder inside your OS X user folder. So, for example, the path to my iTunes music files would be chris/Music/iTunes/iTunes Music.

  Windows users will find their iTunes Music folder by following this path: yourusername/My Music/iTunes/iTunes Music.

  You can also add compatible videos and movies to your iTunes Library by these means. Those videos will most likely appear in the Movies playlist in the Source list.

  I say "most likely" because in some cases, they may instead appear in the Music or TV Shows playlist. Videos that are specifically designated as Music Videos will appear in the Music playlist. Similarly, videos that are specifically designated as TV shows will appear in the TV Shows playlist. Later in the chapter, I'll talk about how to "tag" a video so this happens.

Create and Configure a Playlist

Before we put any music and videos on your iPod, let's organize them in iTunes. Doing so will make it far easier to find the music and videos you want, both in iTunes and on your little portable pal. The best way to organize that material is through the use of playlists.

A *playlist* is simply a group of tracks and videos that you believe should be gathered together in a list. The organizing principle is completely up to you. You can organize songs by artist, by mood, by style, by song length ... heck, if you like, you can create a playlist based on tracks that contain the letter z and a prime number. And you can organize your videos by director, actor, or TV series. In the case of music videos, you can plunk those videos in with music tracks by the same artist. As far as playlists are concerned, you're the boss. Let's look at ways to create those playlists.

Standard playlists

Standard playlists are those that you make by hand. To create one in iTunes, follow these steps:

1. Click the large plus-sign (+) button in the bottom-left corner of the iTunes window, or choose File > New Playlist (Command-N on the Mac, Ctrl+N in Windows).

2. Enter a name for your new playlist in the high-lighted field that appears next to that new play-list in the Source list (**Figure 3.6**).

Figure 3.6
Naming a new
playlist.

3. Click an appropriate entry in the Source list—Music, Movies, TV Shows, or Podcasts—and select the tracks or videos you want to place in the play-list you created.

4. Drag the selected tracks or videos to the new playlist's icon.

Video Playlists vs. Music Playlists

On the iPod, playlists that contain video operate a little differently from music-only playlists. It's like this:

- Playlists that contain only videos will appear in the Video Playlists screen (Videos > Video Playlists > *nameofplaylist*).

- Playlists that include at least one music video and at least one music track will appear both in the Video Playlists screen and in the Music Playlists screen (Music > Playlists > *nameofplaylist*). In such cases, if you choose the music video in a music playlist, it will play the audio from the music video but not the video. If you choose the music video in the video playlist, you can watch the video as well as hear the soundtrack.

- Nonmusic videos—videos designated as Movies, TV Shows, and Video Podcasts by iTunes—won't appear in a music playlist on the iPod even though you may have included such videos when creating the playlist in iTunes.

5. After you've dragged the material you want into your playlist, arrange its order: Click the Number column in the main window, and drag tracks up and down in the list.

When the iPod is synchronized with iTunes, this is the order in which the songs will appear in the playlist on your iPod.

If the songs in your playlist come from the same album, and you want the songs in the playlist to appear in the same order in which they do on the original album, click the Album heading.

Playlist from Selection

You can also create a new playlist from selected items by following these steps:

1. Select the songs and/or videos you'd like to appear in the new playlist.

2. Choose File > New Playlist from Selection (Command-Shift-N on a Mac; there's no keyboard shortcut for this in the Windows version of iTunes).

A new playlist containing the selected items will appear under the Playlists heading in the iTunes Source list. If all selected tracks are from the same album, the list will bear the name of the artist and album. If the tracks are from different albums by the same artist, the playlist will be named after the artist. If you've mixed tracks from different albums or music tracks and videos, a new playlist bearing the name "untitled play-list" will appear.

3. To name (or rename) the playlist, type in the highlighted field.

Smart Playlists

Smart Playlists are slightly different beasts. These playlists include tracks that meet certain conditions you've defined—for example, OutKast tracks encoded in AAC format that are shorter than 4 minutes. Here's how to work the magic of Smart Playlists:

1. In iTunes, choose File > New Smart Playlist (Command-Option-N on the Mac, Ctrl+Alt+N in Windows).

You can also hold down the Option key on the Mac or the Shift key on a Windows PC and click the Gear icon that replaces the Plus button at the bottom of the iTunes window.

2. Choose your criteria.

You'll spy a pop-up menu that allows you to select items by various criteria—including artist, composer, genre, podcast, bit rate, comment, date added, and last played—followed by a Contains field. To choose all songs by Elvis Presley and Elvis Costello, for example, you'd choose Artist from the pop-up menu and then enter **Elvis** in the Contains field.

You can limit the selections that appear in the playlist by minutes, hours, megabytes, gigabytes, or number of songs. You may want the playlist to contain no more than 5 GB worth of songs and videos, for example.

You'll also see a Live Updating option. When it's switched on, this option ensures that if you add any songs or videos to iTunes that meet the criteria you've set, those files will be added to the playlist. If you add a new Elvis Costello album to iTunes, for example, iTunes updates your Elvis Smart Playlist automatically.

3. Click OK.

A new playlist that contains your smart selections appears in iTunes' Source list.

You don't have to settle for a single criterion. By clicking the plus-sign (+) button next to a criterion field, you can add other conditions. You could create a playlist that contains only songs that you've never listened to by punk artists whose names contain the letter *J*.

iTunes includes six Smart Playlists: 90's Music, My Top Rated, Recently Added, Recently Played, and Top 25 Most Played, and Music Videos. These playlists have the Live Updating option enabled, which makes it possible for them to update dynamically as conditions change (when you rate more songs, play different tunes, or play other tunes more often, for example).

To see exactly what makes these playlists tick, Mac users can Control-click (or right-click) a Smart Playlist and choose Edit Smart Playlist from the resulting contextual menu. Windows users simply right-click a playlist to see this command.

note **In iTunes 4.5, Apple enhanced the Smart Playlist feature in an important way: Now you can tell Smart Playlists to harvest songs only within certain playlists.**

Organize playlists in folders

You can also file playlists in folders. By invoking the File > New Folder command (Shift-Option-Command-N for the Mac and Shift+Ctrl+N in Windows), you can lump a bunch of playlists into a single folder. Folders are a great way to keep your playlists separate from your spouse's or to gather groups of similar playlists (All My Jazz Playlists, for example).

Folders don't translate to the iPod, however, as it's incapable of creating nested folders. When you move a folder full of playlists into the iPod, all the songs within all those playlists appear in a single playlist that bears the folder's name.

Move Music and Video to the iPod (shuffle Excluded)

The next few pages don't apply to the iPod shuffle, as its iTunes interface is significantly different from the one used for other iPod models. Because it is so different, I've chosen to devote the latter portion of this chapter to the shuffle. And because only the 5G iPod supports video, all instructions for moving videos apply to the 5G iPod exclusively.

Now that your media is organized, it's time to put it on your 'pod. The conduit for moving music, podcasts, audiobooks, and videos to the iPod is iTunes—which, fortunately, can be fairly flexible in the way it goes about the process.

By default, any tracks in your iTunes Library—and videos, in the case of the 5G iPod—will be transferred automatically to the iPod when the iPod is plugged into your computer. If there are more tracks in your iTunes Library than will fit on the iPod, iTunes asks permission to create a subset of your music files and then transfers that subset to your iPod.

There are several ways to configure iTunes so that your iPod is updated when you want it to be. It's just as possible to configure iTunes so that only the music and videos you want are copied to your iPod. The key is the iPod Preferences window.

To start, plug your iPod into your computer, and launch iTunes. (By default, iTunes launches when you connect the iPod.) The iPod appears under the Devices heading in iTunes' Source list (**FIGURE 3.7**). To open the iPod Preferences window, select the iPod in the Source list.

Figure 3.7 My iPod in the Source list.

Within the iPod Preferences window, you'll find eight panes if you have a 5G iPod: Summary, Music, Movies, TV Shows, Podcasts, Photos, Contacts, and Games. If you have a color iPod that doesn't offer video (including an iPod nano), the Movies, TV Shows, and Games tabs will be absent. For monochrome iPods, the Photos tab will be missing.

Below these tabs, you'll see the Capacity gauge (**FIGURE 3.8**). This is a thermometerlike display that details how much media is on your iPod. With a 5G iPod, you'll see entries for Audio, Video, Photos, Other (read: data like files you've copied to the iPod, notes, contacts, and calendars), and Free Space. Click the gauge, and the display cycles through amounts of storage used by each kind of media (measured in GB and MB); the numbers of items of each kind of media (7,660 songs, 109 videos, and 6,098 photos, for example); and how long it would take to play the audio and video files (26.6 days, for example).

Figure 3.8 The Capacity gauge.

Here's how the panes shake out.

Summary

In iTunes 7, the Summary pane provides such details about your iPod as its name, capacity, software version number, serial number, and format. It also will tell you the version of the iPod software it's running and offer you the option to update that software if newer software is available or restore your iPod (essentially, erase its contents and give it a new operating system). I'll cover the ins and outs of restoring your iPod in Chapter 8.

Finally, the Summary tab offers these options.

Open iTunes When This iPod Is Connected

Most likely, you're going to want to sync or otherwise muck with your iPod when you plug it into your computer. This option saves you the trouble of launching iTunes manually.

Only Sync Checked Items

This provides fine control over which files you sync to the iPod. Checking the box for this option lets you prevent files from loading onto the iPod by unchecking the small check boxes next to their names in playlists and Library lists.

tip

Care to check or uncheck all the songs in a playlist at the same time? On the Mac, hold down the Command key and click any check box in the playlist. In Windows, hold down the Control key and do the same thing. When you uncheck a box, all boxes will be unchecked; check a box, and all boxes will be checked.

Manually Manage Music (and Videos, on 5G iPods)

This small option offers a lot of power. To understand its usefulness, it's helpful to know that by default, when you sync iTunes and the iPod, iTunes moves only the files you ask it for onto the iPod and erases everything else from the device. This can be a real bother if you've moved your iPod from one computer to another, and the contents of the second computer don't match those of the first.

Managing files manually allows you to add music (and videos, for compatible iPods) to your iPod without erasing any other media. When you select this option, all the playlists on your iPod appear below the iPod's icon in the iTunes Source list. (For the sake of simplicity, we'll say that the Music, Movies, TV Shows, Podcasts, and Audiobooks entries count as playlists.)

To add media files to the iPod manually, just select them in one of iTunes' playlists, and drag them to the iPod's icon in the Source list or to one of the iPod's standard (not Smart) playlists (**FIGURE 3.9**). You can also drag files from your computer's desktop directly to the iPod, which copies the media to the iPod but not to your iTunes Library.

Figure 3.9
Moving music
to the iPod
manually.

Optionally, you can add songs by genre, artist, or album by using iTunes' browser. To do so, follow these steps:

1. In iTunes, choose Edit > Show Browser (Command-B in Mac OS X; Ctrl+B in Windows).

A pane divided into Genre, Artist, and Album columns appears at the top of iTunes' main window.

2. Click an entry in one of the columns.

If you want to copy all the Kate Bush songs in your iTunes Library to the iPod, for example, click Ms. Bush's name in the Artist column. To copy all the reggae tunes to the iPod, select Reggae in the Genre column.

3. Drag the selected item to the iPod's icon in the Source list or to a playlist you've created on the iPod.

To remove songs from the iPod, select the songs you want to remove within the iPod entry in the Source list; then press your keyboard's Delete key (or Control-click on the Mac or right-click for Windows, and choose Clear from the contextual menu). Mac users can also drag the songs to the Trash.

tip When you remove songs from your iPod, you don't remove them from your computer. Unless you select a song in iTunes' Library and delete it, the song is still on your hard drive.

You can even copy entire playlists to other playlists by dragging one playlist icon on top of another. This method works for both iTunes and iPod playlists, though you can't drag a playlist on the iPod to an iTunes playlist and expect the songs to copy over. Under most circumstances, tracks on the iPod don't copy to your computer (unless you know the tricks detailed in Chapter 7).

Figure 3.10
iTunes' View
buttons.

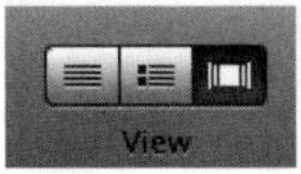

But wait—there's more. iTunes 7 includes two new views: Album and CoverFlow view. To see your music in each of these views, click the second button in the View palette at the top of the window to see the Album view. The CoverFlow view appears when you click the third button (**Figure 3.10**). As their names hint, these views let you see your music by album cover.

Specifically, in Album view, you'll see the artwork
for any album available from the iTunes Store on
the left side of the window and the contents of that
album on the right (**FIGURE 3.11**). CoverFlow is kind
of a lazy-Susan affair that represents your library as
a series of covers (**FIGURE 3.12**). You can move music
from these views to your iPod simply by dragging
the cover art from the view to the iPod's icon. The
contents of that album, video, or podcast will be
transferred to the iPod.

Figure 3.11
Album view.

Figure 3.12
CoverFlow view.

When you choose to manage your songs and playlists manually, you'll be told that you have to disconnect the iPod manually—meaning that you have to take action to unmount the thing, rather than simply unplug it from your computer. To do so, you can click the Eject icon next to the iPod's name in the Source list, or select the iPod and then click the small icon of the iPod that appears in the bottom-right corner of the iTunes window. Alternatively, Mac users can switch to the Finder and drag the iPod to the Trash. When its icon disappears from the Desktop, you can unplug your iPod. Windows users can invoke the Safely Remove Hardware command from the system tray. If you unmount the iPod by doing something rash like unplugging it, your computer's operating system will complain, and your iPod may not have all the media you wanted it to have if it was busy doing something.

The iPod will also tell you when it's ready to be unmounted. When the iPod is mounted on your computer or busy accepting data from an application, its display flashes the international symbol for "Back off, Jack!" (the circle with a line through it), along with a "Do not disconnect" message. When you unmount it properly, the iPod displays its main menu.

Enable Disk Use

The iPod is, at heart, an elegant storage device that happens to play music and, in some cases, slideshows and videos. You can mount the iPod as a hard drive on your computer by enabling this option. When the iPod is mounted, you can use it just like a hard drive; copy files to it as you desire.

Music

The Music pane (**Figure 3.13**) contains options for syncing music and music videos to your iPod, as well as for displaying album artwork on a color iPod.

Figure 3.13 The Music pane.

Enabling the Sync Music option tells iTunes that you'd like it to sync its music collection to the iPod automatically. If you've enabled the Manually Manage Music and Videos option in the Summary pane, enabling the Sync Music option overrides the Manual option (iTunes will ask you if you're sure you want to do this). When you've chosen Sync Music, you then have the choice to sync all songs and playlists or just selected playlists.

Any songs currently on the iPod that aren't in the iTunes Library or in the selected playlists are erased from the iPod.

Why choose selected playlists rather than your entire music library? For one thing, your iPod may not have the capacity to hold your entire music collection. This option is also a good one to use when several members of your family share an iPod. It allows you to chunk up a music collection into multiple playlists and then rotate those playlists in and out of the iPod.

If you've removed songs from the iTunes Library and want them to remain on your iPod after the update, you'll want to avoid this option and manage your music manually.

Movies (5G iPod only)

The Movies pane (**FIGURE 3.14**) is similar to the Music pane. Here, you'll find the option to Sync Movies and then choices to sync All Movies, All Unwatched Movies, All Most Recent Unwatched Movies (this can be 1, 3, 5, or 10 most recent unwatched movies), or Selected Movies or Selected Playlists. iTunes provides this greater level of sync control because movies take up a lot of space, and a large movie collection and even the highest-capacity iPod may not mix.

Figure 3.14 The Movies pane.

Again, if you enable the Sync Movies option, you undo the Manually Manage Movies and Videos setting if you've switched it on.

TV Shows (5G iPod only)

The TV Shows pane (**Figure 3.15**) also provides greater flexibility than does the Music pane. Here, you can choose to sync all TV shows; 1, 3, 5, or 10 of the most recent; all unwatched TV shows; 1, 3, 5, or 10 of the most recent unwatched TV shows; or the selected TV shows or playlists.

Figure 3.15 The TV Shows pane.

Echoing my past statements, if you allow syncing of your TV shows, you disable the Manually Manage Movies and Videos setting.

Podcasts

It would be pretty silly to own a music player called the iPod that didn't play podcasts. Yours does, and this pane determines how podcasts are treated by iTunes and the iPod (**Figure 3.16**).

Much like with the TV Shows pane, you can choose to sync all episodes of all podcasts; 1, 3, 5, or 10 most recent of all your subscribed podcasts; all unplayed podcasts you subscribe to; or 1, 3, 5, or 10 of the

most recent unplayed episodes of all your podcasts.
Alternatively, you can use these same options with
selected podcasts rather than all your subscribed
podcasts.

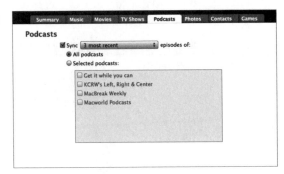

Figure 3.16 The
Podcasts pane.

Photos (color iPods only)

If you have a color iPod, you can synchronize pictures
between your photo library and your iPod. The key
to doing so is within the Photos pane of the iPod
Preferences window.

Sync Photos From option

When you enable this option, you'll see an alert that
asks whether you're really sure you want to enable
photo support. iTunes does this to warn you that any
photos currently on the iPod will be replaced. You
don't have the option to manage photos manually;
thus, you have to be more careful about accidentally
erasing pictures when you plug your color iPod into
another computer.

With this option enabled, you can choose a source
for your photos. On a Macintosh, you'll see iPhoto
listed in the Sync Photos From pop-up menu (**Figure
3.17**); you also have the option to choose images from
the Pictures folder in your user folder or to select any
other folder. This works pretty much as you'd expect.

Figure 3.17 The
Photos pane.

When you choose iPhoto, the option below the pop-
up menu reads All Photos and Albums. When you
enable this option, all the pictures in your iPhoto
library will be converted and copied to the iPod. You
also have the option Selected Albums, which works
much like the Selected Playlists option in the Music
pane. Regardless of which option you choose, whenever you add new images to a selected album, the
iPod automatically updates its photo library when it
next synchronizes.

If you choose Pictures from this pop-up menu, the
options below it change to All Photos and Selected
Folders. The principles of iPhoto import apply here
as well. If you choose All Photos, iTunes rummages
around in this folder and looks for compatible graphics

files. If you choose Selected Folders, you can direct iTunes to look in only those folders that you select.

Finally, you can select Choose Folder. When you do, up pops a Change Photos Folder Location navigation window. Just traipse to the folder you want to pull pictures from, and click Choose. When you do this, the folder you've chosen replaces Pictures in the pop-up menu.

tip **This is a good way to copy every picture from your hard drive to your iPod. As far as iTunes is concerned, your hard drive is just another folder. Select it as the source folder with the All Photos option selected, and iTunes grabs all the compatible graphics files it can find, converts them, and plunks them onto your iPod.**

This process is no more complicated for Windows users. The main difference is that the Windows version of iTunes offers no iPhoto option (and because there is no version of iPhoto for Windows, that's probably a good thing). Instead, you'll see the option to sync All or Selected Folders from your My Pictures folder or another folder of your choosing.

If you've installed Adobe Photoshop Elements (version 3 or later) or Adobe Photoshop Album on your PC, the Sync Photos From pop-up menu also contains entries for these programs, allowing you to import pictures from the albums these programs create.

tip **The tip I proposed for copying all the pictures from your Mac to your iPod works with Windows as well. In this case, choose your C drive as the source. When you do, every compatible graphics file will be converted and copied.**

Include Full-Resolution Photos

Near the bottom of the Photos pane you'll see the Include Full-Resolution Photos option, followed by this text:

Copy full-resolution versions of your photos into the Photos folder on your iPod, which you can access after enabling disk use.

This is a useful hunk of text, in that it hints at where your full-resolution images are stored, but if space permitted, it would be even more useful if it continued with these words:

Oh, and don't get your hopes up thinking that just because you've copied these full-resolution images to your iPod, you'll be able to view these exact images on your iPod or project them on a television. No, sir (or madam, as the case may be), this option is provided only as a convenient way to transfer your images to the iPod so that you can later attach it to a different computer and copy your pictures from here to there.

note **The Full Resolution folder, which appears within the iPod's Photos folder, is organized in a logical way. When you open the Full Resolution folder, you'll see a folder that bears the year the pictures were created. Within this folder are folders marked with the month of creation. Within one of these folders is a folder denoting the day of conception. So the folder hierarchy might look like this: Photos/Full Resolution/2007/2/28/yourphotos.**

Contacts

iTunes handles synchronization of contacts and calendars between your computer and iPod. The Contacts pane offers synchronization options for your computer's main contacts and calendars applications. From the Contacts pane on a Macintosh, you can choose to synchronize all your Apple Address Book contacts or just those contacts from selected groups. On a Windows PC, iTunes synchronizes Windows' Address Book or Microsoft Outlook contacts in the same way—either all contacts or selected groups of contacts. Only in the Macintosh version of iTunes do you also have the option to include the photo associated with your contact.

Below the Contacts section of the pane, you'll spy the Calendars section. This works similarly to Contacts. On a Mac, you can sync all your iCal calendars or just selected calendars. On a Windows PC, you have these same options for Microsoft Outlook calendars.

Move Music to the iPod shuffle

As I mentioned earlier in the chapter, the iPod shuffle interacts differently with iTunes than does a display-bearing iPod. To begin with, because the shuffle lacks a screen, there's no need to offer options for synchronizing photos, videos, contacts, and calendars. The lack of a screen also means that there's little you can do to navigate a shuffle's music library. You are, in a very real sense, flying blind.

And then there's the shuffle's limited storage space. Because the current shuffles hold just 1 GB (and a previous model held only 512 MB), you don't have a lot of extra room for storing large music files. iTunes does its best to keep such files from being placed on your music player automatically.

With these limitations in mind, let's take a look at just what iTunes offers for the shuffle owner.

When you attach an iPod shuffle to your Mac or PC, by default, iTunes launches. When it does, the shuffle appears in the iTunes Source list under the Devices heading just like any other iPod (save for the fact that its icon looks like a shuffle rather than a full-size iPod). Select that shuffle, and iTunes' main window shows two tabs: Settings and Contents, with the Contents tab front and center.

Contents tab

In the top part of the window, you see a list of tracks you've loaded on the shuffle. At the bottom of the window, you see the Autofill pane (**FIGURE 3.18**), which contains the following items:

Figure 3.18 The shuffle's Autofill pane.

Autofill button

In theory, putting music on your shuffle is very simple. By default, iTunes is set up so that when you click the Autofill button, iTunes grabs a collection of random tracks from your iTunes Library and copies it to your shuffle. But things don't have to work that way. Although the Autofill button, in league with the Autofill From pop-up menu (which you'll hear about in just a sec), is a powerful way to move music to your shuffle, you need never touch it.

Blasphemy? Perhaps. But the only way to ensure that you get *exactly* the music you want on your shuffle is to lay off this button. Instead, if your shuffle has anything on it, select it, select all its contents, and press your computer's Delete key. Then drag just the music you want from your iTunes Library onto the shuffle's icon.

To see the order in which songs will play if the shuffle is set to play from beginning to end, click the Number heading in iTunes' main window. To save that playlist so that you don't lose it when you later fill your shuffle with other music, select everything in the playlist, and choose File > New Playlist from Selection. A new playlist will be created in iTunes' Source list that includes all the selected tracks.

If you choose to bang the Autofill button, of course, it will do exactly what it says: fill your shuffle with as much as it can of the playlist selected in the Autofill From pop-up menu.

Autofill From pop-up menu

One way to customize your shuffle's contents more carefully is to feed it from specific playlists. You might create sets of music that make sense for particular activities—music for your next workout or for a car trip, for example. When you've created these playlists, you can choose the one you like from the Autofill From pop-up menu.

Choose Items Randomly

The shuffle was designed with random play in mind, but you can make it load specific tracks in a specific order by disabling this option. When you do, iTunes will take the playlist selected in the Autofill From pop-up menu and place as much of it as can fit, in order, on the shuffle. When you've flipped your shuffle into "play from beginning to end" mode, the playlist you load will play in that order. This is one way to ensure that the songs in an album you place on the shuffle play in the same order as they do on the album.

Choose Higher Rated Items More Often

I mean, honestly, what's the use of putting music or podcasts that you loathe on your shuffle? If you haven't thought of a good reason for rating your audio files, now you have one. Assign a rating of four or five stars to your favorite tracks, and those tracks are more likely to be moved to your shuffle when this option is enabled.

Replace All Items When Autofilling

When this option is selected, iTunes will wipe out whatever music the shuffle currently holds and replace it with selections from the playlist chosen in the Autofill From pop-up menu. Leaving this box checked is a good way to help ensure that you'll get a fresh crop of music the next time you listen to your shuffle. It's not such a good choice, however, if you want to keep some selections on the shuffle—podcasts, for example—and remove others.

Uncheck this option and check Only Update Checked Songs in the Settings tab (which we'll get to very shortly), and you've got a whole lot more control. This way, you can uncheck all your podcasts (or other tracks you want to keep) on the shuffle and then click the Autofill button. The stuff you want to keep stays put and is surrounded by new material.

Settings tab

The other tab you see when selecting an iPod shuffle in the Source list provides settings for formatting the little devil and managing its relationship with iTunes. The Settings tab (**Figure 3.19**) includes the some of the same options you find in a display-bearing iPod's Summary pane.

Figure 3.19
The shuffle's
Settings tab.

At the top of the pane, you'll find information regarding the shuffle's name, capacity, software version number, and serial number.

Below is the same Version area that you see for other iPods. Here, you can update or restore your iPod with the latest iPod software.

The Options area is where the good stuff happens. Here, you'll see options for launching iTunes when the shuffle is attached, updating only checked songs, converting higher-bit-rate songs to 128 Kbps AAC, enabling Sound Check, and enabling disk use. You're familiar with some of these options already. Let's look at the new ones.

Convert Higher Bit Rate Songs to 128 Kbps AAC

Although the shuffle can play uncompressed files (which you learned about earlier in the chapter), on a device with such limited storage, it's not a good idea to pack it with these large files. Enabling this option instructs iTunes to slim down stout files so that they take up less space on the shuffle.

iTunes won't automatically place Apple Lossless files on your shuffle; on the 1G shuffle, it also won't load AIFF files. If you drag such files to the shuffle to place them on the player manually, however, iTunes will automatically convert them to 128 Kbps AAC files when this option is enabled. Your files will remain in their original format on your computer, but compressed copies will be made just for the shuffle.

Enable Sound Check

You may recall from Chapter 2 that Sound Check is a feature that attempts to play all the songs in iTunes at the same volume. Enable this option, and your shuffle will use those Sound Check settings to play back tracks at a fairly consistent volume.

Limit Maximum Volume

I covered this in Chapter 2 as well. Enable the option, and adjust the slider to set a maximum volume for the shuffle. Click the Lock icon to password-protect this option.

Enable Disk Use

If you enable this option, you can mount the shuffle on your computer and use it to store data files as well as music files.

To help ensure that you've got some room left for data files, iTunes includes a slider below this option that allows you to determine how much of the shuffle's storage space will be reserved for songs and how much will go toward data storage. If you set the slider to the halfway point on a 512 MB iPod shuffle, you can fit approximately 60 4-minute 128 Kbps AAC songs and 156 MB of data on your iPod. Double those figures for a 1 GB shuffle.

Tag, You're It

So how does iTunes know about tracks, artists, albums, and genres? Through something called *ID3 tags*. ID3 tags are just little bits of data included in a song file that tell programs like iTunes something about the file—not just the track's name and the album it came from, but also the composer, the album track number, the year it was recorded, and whether it is part of a compilation.

These ID3 tags are the key to creating great Smart Playlists. To view this information, select a track, and choose File > Get Info. Click the Info tab in the resulting window, and you'll see fields for all kinds of things. You may find occasions when it's helpful to change the information in these fields. If you have two versions of the same song—perhaps one is a studio recording, and another is a live recording—you could change the title of the latter to include (*Live*).

A really useful field to edit is the Comments field. Here, you can enter anything you like and then use that entry to sort your music. If a particular track would be great to fall asleep to, for example, enter **sleepy** in the Comments field. Do likewise with similar tracks, and when you're ready to hit the hay, create a Smart Playlist that includes "Comment is sleepy." With this technique under your belt, you can create playlists that fit particular moods or situations, such as a playlist that gets you pumped up during a workout.

4

The iTunes Store

In Chapter 3, you learned how to put the music and video you own on your iPod. Now it's time to look at a cool way to obtain new media. And by *cool*, I can mean nothing other than Apple's online digital media emporium, the iTunes Store. In the following pages, I'll take you on a tour of The Store and show you the best ways to discover and purchase new media.

The One-Stop Shop

Apple has eschewed the typical Internet-commerce model of creating a Web site that users access through a Web browser. Although this model works reasonably well for countless merchants, it invariably requires customers to slog through Web page after Web page to find and pay for the items they desire. Apple wanted a service as immediate as the experience of going to a media megastore, gathering the music and movies you want, and taking them to the counter.

To replicate this experience, Apple placed The Store inside an application that was already built for music browsing (and, later, video browsing) and that many of its customers were likely to be familiar with: iTunes.

Incorporating The Store into iTunes offered several benefits:

- It's easy to access. Just open iTunes and click the iTunes Store entry in the Source list. If your computer is connected to the Internet, the iTunes Store interface appears in the main iTunes window.

tip Starting with iTunes 4.6, Apple made visiting The Store even easier (or, some may say, more annoying). The first time you connect your iPod to your computer or restore your iPod, iTunes launches and displays the iTunes Store page. To stop it from doing so, simply click the small X in the information window at the top of the iTunes window, and select a different item in iTunes' Source list.

- It's a cinch to find music, audiobooks, podcasts, music videos, TV shows, and movies. First, enter a search term in the Search iTunes Store field, located in the top-right corner of the iTunes window. (This term can be pretty much anything you like: artist, album, song title, podcast title, TV show, movie, even a single word.) Then press the Mac's Return key or the PC's Enter key. In very little time, a window appears that's partitioned into categories containing items that match your query: Albums, Artists, Music Videos, TV Shows, Movies, Podcasts, and Audiobooks. If you type **Louie** in the search field, for example, you'll see links to a few albums (including *The Best of the Kingsmen*, due to their perennial frat-house favorite "Louie Louie"), as well as music videos by the artist Louie Louie, an audiobook by Louie Giglio, and an HBO podcast for the show "Lucky Louie."

- It's hard to get lost. Should you ever wander into one of the scarier sections of The Store (say, the polka aisle), it's easy to find your way back to the main page. Simply click the Home icon at the top of the iTunes window, and you're transported to the main page.

  Next to the Home icon, you'll see a path from your present location to the main page—Home/Rock/Peter Gabriel/Secret World Live, for example. To move up a level or two, simply click one of the entries in this hierarchy.

  Another way to retrace your steps is to use the Back and Forward buttons, just to the left of the

Home icon. These buttons are similar to the Back and Forward buttons in your Web browser. Click the Back button to move to the page you viewed previously. If you've backtracked and want to go forward again, click the Forward button.

- It's tough to purchase media you don't want. The Store allows you to sample a 30-second preview of every song, music video, and TV show it sells. Audiobooks get a 90-second preview. And movies offer the theatrical trailer you'd see in a theatre. Highlight the item you want to preview; then click iTunes' Play button, Preview (audiobooks), or View Trailer (movies).

- It couldn't be much easier to purchase media. Simply create an Apple account, locate the media you want to buy, and click the Buy button next to the pertinent item. After iTunes confirms your decision to purchase, it downloads the item to your computer. Songs cost, on average, 99 cents apiece; albums, $9.99; and music videos and TV shows, $1.99 each. Movies come in three prices. "Library" (read: older) movies are $9.99; preorder and movies released during the current week are $12.99; and current movies that are more than a week old are $14.99. Audiobooks can be priced from a little to a lot, and podcasts are free.

- Finally, when the media is on your computer, you can copy it to your iPod (video will play only on 5G iPods, of course) and play it on up to five computers. You can burn music to an audio CD that you can play anywhere you like. You can't burn any variety of video to a disc that can be played in a commercial DVD player. Instead, Apple allows you to burn music videos, TV shows, and movies as data for the purposes of backup (in other words, you're just copying the video files so you can restore them to your computer if something should happen to the original). You can do all this without leaving the iTunes application.

In short, the entire process is about as complicated as ordering and eating a Big Mac and fries (and a whole lot healthier!). Easy to use as it may be, however, The Store has hidden depths. In the following pages, I'll explain all that there is to know about The Store, and tell you how you and your iPod can put it to the best use.

Prepare to Shop

Ready to shop? Great. Let's make sure that you have the tools you need to get started. After you have those tools, we'll get you signed up with an account and then take an extensive tour of The Store.

What you need

Of course, you need a Mac or Windows PC and a copy of iTunes. Although it's not necessary to have an iPod to take advantage of The Store—media purchased at The Store can be played on your computer, and music can be burned to CD—the iPod technically is the only portable media player capable of playing music purchased at The Store.

And although you can access The Store via any Internet connection, you'll find it far more fun to shop with a broadband connection. A 4-minute song weighs in at around 4 MB. Such a download over a DSL or cable connection takes next to no time at all but can be terribly slow over a poky modem connection. And even with a DSL or cable connection, you could wait up to an hour to download a full-length movie from The Store.

As these pages go to print, The Store is available in 21 countries. Which store you're allowed to purchase media from depends on the issuing country of your credit card. If you have a credit card issued in Germany, for example, you can purchase media only from the German iTunes Store (though you don't physically have to be in Germany to do this—again, the credit card determines where you can shop).

Signing on

You're welcome to browse The Store the first time you fire up iTunes, but to purchase media, you must establish an account and sign in. Fortunately, Apple makes it pretty easy to do so. The process goes like this:

With your computer connected to the Internet, launch iTunes, and click the iTunes Store entry in iTunes' Source list; then click the Sign In button in the top-right corner of the iTunes window. If you have either an Apple ID and password or an AOL screen name and password, enter them and click the Sign In button; otherwise, click the Create Account button.

When creating an account, you'll need to enter a valid email address and create a password. After you've done these things, you'll enter some personal information so that Apple can identify you, if need be.

Finally, after you've traipsed through The Store's terms and conditions, you'll be asked for a credit-card number and your name, address, and phone number. Click Done and ... well, you're done. You're now a member in good standing.

Navigate The Store's Floors

As I tap out these words, The Store carries more than 3.5 million songs, 65,000 podcasts, 20,000 audio-books, 200 TV shows, fewer than a hundred movies, and a fistful of iPod games. Fortunately, you needn't trudge through an alphabetical list of all these titles. Instead, Apple offers you multiple ways to browse its catalog of goodies. Let's look at The Store's floor plan and the best ways to navigate it.

The Store's main page offers a host of links for finding the media you desire (**Figure 4.1**). Much like a "real" media megastore, The Store places the day's most popular picks up front.

Across the top of the main page, you'll see a banner that changes from time to time. This banner may promote hot new singles or albums, exclusive tracks, music videos, TV shows, and movies.

Below the banner are tabbed, side-scrolling panes. The topmost pane offers tabs for new releases in the Music, Movies, and TV Shows categories, along

with three additional music tabs to fill out the pane:
Rock, Alternative, and Pop. When you choose one of
the music tabs, you can view eight items within the
pane. Click the arrow icons on either side of the pane
to view more items in this category. The Movies and
TV Shows tabs present this material in a view similar
to iTunes' CoverFlow view.

Figure 4.1
The Store's
main page.

Below New Releases, you'll see What's Hot, Staff
Favorites, Exclusively on iTunes, and Free on iTunes.
Some of these panes include tabs, and others don't.
Sandwiched between these panes are links to things
like just-added items, the free music download of
the week, a celebrity playlist, and ads for movies
and iPods. (Note that Apple rejiggers The Store's
interface pretty regularly, so this description may not
exactly match what you see the next time you visit
The Store.)

tip On a slowish connection, it takes a while for these panes to refresh and lists to scroll. You can scan the contents of these panes far more quickly if you click the See All link in the top-right corner of each pane.

Arrayed along the top-left side of the main page are text links that direct you to many of The Store's most interesting features, described in the following sections.

iTunes Store

In this box, placed in the upper-left corner of The Store's main page, you choose the kind of media you want to browse—music, movies, TV shows, music videos, audiobooks, podcasts, or iPod games (**FIGURE 4.2**). When you click one of these links, you're taken to the main page for that kind of media. These pages are similar to The Store's main page—offering lists of top-selling items within that category and highlighting new releases, for example.

Figure 4.2
Narrow your media search via the iTunes Store links.

iTunes STORE
Music
Movies NEW
TV Shows
Music Videos
Audiobooks
Podcasts
iPod Games NEW

Music

Longtime iTunes Store customers may fear that some of their old favorite features—iMix, iTunes Originals, iTunes Essentials, Collections, and Celebrity Playlist, for example—have disappeared simply because they've vanished from The Store's main page. Fear not. The music-centric items have been moved to the More in Music area of the main Music page. For those unfamiliar with these features, here's how the most significant music features shake out:

iTunes Collections Clicking iTunes Collections takes you to something like a "greatest music hits of The Store" page. Here, you find links to best-selling iTunes Essentials collections (more on these in the next couple of pages); featured "The World Of" artist collections; iTunes Live Sessions (live recordings sold exclusively at the iTunes Store); and Where You From?, collections of regional recordings.

iMix iMix is your chance to inflict your musical values on the rest of the world by publishing a playlist of your favorite (or, heck, your least-favorite) songs. When you click the iMix link, you're taken to a page that contains three columns marked Top Rated, Most Recent, and Featured, all listing iMix playlists posted by fellow music lovers. Type a genre, artist name, or keyword (like summer or drive) in the Search For field to narrow your choices, or just click an "album cover" to view the songs in an iMix (and buy them, if you like).

As enjoyable as it may be to view others' iMixes, it's more fun to create your own. You can do so by following these steps:

1. Create a new playlist in iTunes, and give it a really cool name.

   The cooler the name, the more likely others are to view your iMix.

2. Cruise through your iTunes Library, and drag into it songs you'd like to publish in an iMix.

   Note that your iMix can contain only songs available for purchase from The Store. If the iMix contains songs that are not available at The Store, those songs won't appear in the published playlist.

3. Round out your list with songs at The Store that you don't own.

   An iMix doesn't require that you actually own the music you're recommending; you can drag previews of any song or audiobook from The Store into a playlist in iTunes' Source list. Feel free to add these previews to your iMix playlist.

4. Click the arrow to the right of your playlist's name.

   When you click this arrow, a dialog box asks whether you'd like to give the playlist as a gift or publish it as an iMix.

5. Click Create iMix.

You'll be asked to sign in with your Apple ID. Then you'll be taken to The Store, and iTunes' main window will show you a picture of your iMix's album cover (a collage of album covers for the songs you've included).

6. Edit the title and description to suit your iMix.

7. Click Publish and then click Done.

Your iMix will be published to The Store and will remain there for 1 year. You'll receive an email confirmation of the iMix's publication and a link to it. Click the link, and iTunes takes you to your iMix's page. Here, you have the option to advertise your link to friends by clicking the Tell a Friend link.

iTunes Originals iTunes Originals are albums created specifically for The Store by such artists as Red Hot Chili Peppers, Mary J. Blige, Ben Harper, and Barenaked Ladies. These albums variously feature bonus cuts, live performances, and interviews in which the artists offer insights into the album's music tracks.

iTunes Essentials Although you can purchase entire albums from The Store (and are occasionally required to purchase an entire album to get all the songs on it), it's mostly a song-based enterprise. By this, I mean that The Store encourages you to pick and choose just the pieces of music you like.

Given this idea, it makes sense that Apple would offer compilations of songs, organized by some catchy sort of theme—Women in Bluegrass,

Animation Classics, or It Came from TV!, for example—or by an artist. Apple calls these compilations iTunes Essentials.

Yes, these are essentially Apple's own iMixes—collections of songs the folks who work at The Store think you'll like (**Figure 4.3**). Unlike most of The Store's other albums, these compilations don't give you a discount. If an iTunes Essential contains 25 songs, you pay $24.75, or 99 cents per song.

Figure 4.3
iTunes
Essentials.

iTunes Essentials are offered in four configurations: The Basics, Next Steps, Deep Cuts, and Complete Set. As their names indicate, The Basics includes the most obvious songs that fit a particular theme; Next Steps offers slightly more obscure tracks; Deep Cuts hits the fringes; and Complete Set offers all songs in the previous three categories.

Celebrity Playlists If you'd like to know what rocks the worlds of Brian Wilson, Toby Keith, Samuel L. Jackson, and Snow Patrol (no, I'm not exactly sure which Patrolman picked the tunes for that particular list), click these links. The resulting page offers a list of tunes an artist thinks worthy. Of course, you can preview and purchase songs—either individually or the entire list—directly from this page.

Nike Sport Music As mentioned earlier in the book, Nike and Apple have teamed to pair music and athletic shoes. This section of The Store features mixes designed for the perfect workout. Each mix includes an opening narration that describes the kind of workout the mix is for, followed by the songs.

Genres Pane Given the links to New Releases, Exclusives, Pre-Releases, Staff Favorites, iTunes Essentials, Celebrity Playlists, and Today's Top Songs and Albums, as well as access to the Search and Browse functions, you should be well on your way, right? Perhaps. But don't leave the main Music page without checking out the Genre links.

These are great tools to use when you're in the mood for a particular style of music. Just click a genre that appeals to you, such as Folk or Dance.

Choosing an item from the Genre pane takes you to a page devoted to that genre. This page is laid out similarly to the main Music page, containing at least a New Releases area and then other areas that are appropriate for that particular genre. Some genre pages include subcategory listings, for example, while others call out subgenres within that genre—New Orleans and Bebop on the Jazz page, for example.

The Today's Top Songs and Today's Top Albums lists change to reflect The Store's most popular songs and albums within that genre. On these pages, you'll also find links to the top 100 songs and top 100 albums for that genre.

Movies, TV Shows, Music Videos

I lump these three together because the main pages for these media types offer the same kind of structure. Somewhere on each page, you'll see featured items, top sellers, new releases, and a categories breakdown—Comedy, Drama, and Kids & Family for movies, for example.

Audiobooks

This part of The Store resembles the Music section more than the sections that sell videos. Here, you'll find new releases broken into Nonfiction and Fiction areas, category listings (Arts & Entertainment, Classics, Romance, and Sci Fi & Fantasy, for example), What's Hot, Popular Authors, and Radio Programs (mostly audiobooks created from National Public Radio broadcasts).

Podcasts

The Store is a conduit for obtaining podcasts—those do-it-yourself, radiolike broadcasts that you've heard so much about. On the Podcasts page, you'll find a host of podcasts vying for your attention. The structure of the page changes so often that I'm not going to detail what you're likely to find here. Just know that you'll probably see a banner across the top that promotes podcasts deemed interesting by Apple; a Today's Top Podcasts list along the right side that lists that week's most popular 'casts; and a Categories sidebar on the left side that allows you to sort through podcasts by theme—Arts & Entertainment, Business, Comedy, and Public Radio, for example.

When you select a podcast, you'll be taken to a page devoted to it. From this page, you can download single episodes (by clicking the Get Episode button that appears to the right of the podcast) or subscribe to the podcast (by clicking the Subscribe button).

When you click Get Episode, iTunes switches to the Podcasts pane, where all your podcasts are listed, and begins downloading the podcast (**Figure 4.4**). You'll see a subject heading for the podcast—KCRW's Le Show, for example—and when you click the triangle next to that heading, you'll view a list of that program's individual shows.

Figure 4.4 The Podcasts pane.

Next to a show's subject heading, you'll spy a Subscribe button. When you click this Subscribe button or the Subscribe button in one of The Store's podcast pages, some previous episodes of the now-subscribed show will appear in the Podcasts pane, accompanied by a Get button that, when clicked, allows you to retrieve the shows. When new episodes become available, iTunes will download them automatically.

If you tire of receiving a particular show, just select its subject heading and click the Unsubscribe button at the bottom of the iTunes window. You'll no longer receive episodes.

iPod Games

What, you mean they're featuring hints on beating Breakout, Parachute, and Music Quiz? No, thank heavens. iTunes 7 introduced iPod Games, color games specifically designed for 5G iPods. Here, you'll find such classic arcade/computer games as Tetris, Pac-Man, Texas Hold 'em, and Mahjong. Click a title, and you're taken to the game's page, where you can learn more about the game and read customer reviews. Click the Preview button to see a video of the game in action (**FIGURE 4.5**). Games currently sell for $4.99 each.

Figure 4.5 iPod games.

Top of the Pops

Want to see lists of the hottest movies, TV shows, music videos, songs, albums, audiobooks, and podcasts available from The Store? The Top boxes arrayed around the edges of The Store's main page offer just that. All these categories, save audiobooks and podcasts, list the day's top 10 items (audiobooks and podcasts list just the top 5). If you care to view the top 100 items in a particular category, simply click the right-pointing arrow on the right side of each category heading.

Quick Links

The two links at the top of the list—Browse and Power Search—hint that there are more efficient ways to find music than clicking the titles you see on The Store's home page.

Browse

The Store offers a view much like the one you see in iTunes when you select a Library entry or a playlist and choose View > Show Browser. (In point of fact, choosing this command produces the same result as clicking the Browse link.) Click Browse, and iTunes' browser columns appear, listing Charts, Radio Charts, Movies, Music Videos, and The Store's various music genres in the leftmost column.

Charts Click Charts, and Chart appears in the second pane, listing Billboard Hot 100, Billboard Top Country, and Billboard Top R&B. Click one of these entries, and you can choose a year in the third pane. Select a year, and you'll see the top tracks for that year from that particular chart in the list below.

Radio Charts Radio Charts works differently. Click this entry, and you'll see a list of cities in the next pane. Choose a city, and a list of radio stations appears to the right. Select a station to view what's getting major rotation on its playlist.

Movies Select Movies, and a list of categories appears to the right—Action & Adventure, Comedy, and Thriller, for example. Choose one of these categories to see a list of movies that match.

Music Videos Music Videos are broken into categories as well—Alternative, Blues, Holiday, Jazz, and Soundtrack, for example. Select a category, and a list of appropriate artists appears to the right. Click an artist to see what he's or she's been up to in front of the cameras.

TV Shows TV Shows is broken down by series— "24," The Daily Show with Jon Stewart," "Desperate Housewives," and "Weeds," for example (**FIGURE 4.6**). Choose a TV show, and if offered, a list of seasons appears to the right. Choose a season to view individual episodes below. (If there aren't multiple seasons, just clicking the name of the show will produce the list of available episodes at the bottom of the window.)

Genre list Finally, the browser includes a list of music genres. Click a genre name, and for most entries, a list of subgenres appears in the second column. (Not all genres offer subgenres.) Click one of the subgenres, and a list of artists appears in the third column. Click an artist's name, and available albums by that artist appear in the last column. Click an album title, and the music contained on that album appears in the Results area below.

Figure 4.6
The Store's no-nonsense browser.

The Results area is divided into columns titled Name, Time, Artist, Album, Genre, and Price, regardless of whether you're looking at music, movies, music videos, or TV shows. You can sort the list by any of these criteria by clicking the appropriate column head. Click Artist, for example, and the list is sorted alphabetically by artist. Click Time, and the list is sorted by shortest to longest playing time.

tip   You'll notice that a right-pointing arrow appears to the right of entries in some of these views. Clicking this arrow allows you to travel to the page devoted to that item—a great way to explore an album or an artist's catalog after searching for a single song, for example.

Power Search

If you want to be a power shopper, you must learn to take advantage of The Store's Power Search function.

When you click the Power Search link on the main page, you're taken to a page where you can get very specific with your search. Along the top of the window you find the All, Music, Movies, TV Shows, Audiobooks, and Podcasts entries. Click the appropriate entry, and the fields below change to reflect search criteria. Choose the Music entry, and you can enter information in the Artist, Composer, Song, and Album fields, as well as select a genre from the Genre pop-up menu. Click Movies, and you can search for Movie Title, Actor, Director, Producer, Year, and Rating (G, PG, PG-13, or R).

How useful is this? If you performed a simple search for the song "Blue Moon" by entering its title in the Search field, you'd be presented with 898 matches. Even if you search by song title, you'll get just over 577 results. Invoke Power Search, however, and you can narrow things down quite nicely.

If you're interested in vocal renditions of "Blue Moon," for example, enter **Blue Moon** in the Song field and then choose Vocal from the Genre pop-up menu. Aha—now you get just 29 matches. Had you entered **Billie Holiday** in the Artist field, you'd have seen only five matches.

Account

Care to view or edit the information Apple has about you and your credit card? Wonder how you've spent your money at The Store? Want to cancel a movie you've preordered? You can do it all here. When you click the Account link, you'll be asked for your iTunes password. Note that you can also move to your Apple Account Information page by clicking your account name at the top of the iTunes window.

Buy & Redeem

Just like a real store, the iTunes Store lets you purchase and redeem gift certificates. It also lets you create a monthly iTunes Store allowance for that someone special. Click this link to be taken to a page where you can do this and more (**Figure 4.7**). The page works this way:

Figure 4.7 Buy & Redeem.

Redeem Code Apple issues custom iTunes cards for different reasons—to members of the press and for specific downloads of particular items (an album that a band is promoting, for example). This area is for redeeming these special cards. Click this Redeem button, and you'll be taken to the Enter Code screen, where you enter a 12-digit code to obtain credits for whatever the card promises.

Redeem iTunes Gift Cards Apple and some retailers sell prepaid iTunes Gift Cards. If you can't obtain a Store account because you lack a credit card or are looking for an easy-to-give gift, one of these cards is a nice way to go. If you've received such a prepaid card and want to redeem it, just click the Redeem button in the Redeem iTunes Gift Cards area, enter the 16-digit code that appears on the back of the card, and click Redeem. In next to no time, your account will be credited.

Buy Allowance An iTunes allowance can best be described as a gift certificate (which I'll describe in a moment) that keeps on giving. After you create an allowance, the recipient of your largesse will have his or her Store credit bumped up by the amount that you've designated (values include $10 to $100 in $10 increments, $150, and $200) on the first day of each month. Just as when you purchase a gift certificate, your credit card will be charged, not the recipient's.

Here's the way:

1. Click the Buy Now button in the Buy Allowance area.

2. In the Set up an iTunes Allowance window before you, you'll be asked to provide your name, the recipient's name, and a value for the monthly allowance. You'll also be given the option to

send the allowance now or wait until the first of the next month. If your recipient doesn't have an Apple ID, you must create one for him or her. Otherwise, enter the ID in the Apple ID field. You can also append a personal message.

3. Click Continue.

You'll be asked to enter your Apple ID and password. Then you move on to the Confirm Your Purchase screen.

4. After you've checked everything twice, click Buy.

The next screen tells you that the allowance has been created.

5. Click Done to return to the Apple Account Information page.

After you've created an allowance, a new Manage Allowances button appears on your Apple Account Information page. When you click this button, you go to the Edit Allowances page, where you can add allowances or suspend or revoke any that you've created. When you revoke an allowance, any balance placed in the account remains; it won't be credited back to you.

If you think you're going to reinstate that allowance—when your daughter starts making her bed again, for example—use the Suspend button. If you click Remove, you won't be able to put that allowance back into service; you must create a new one. To reactive a suspended account, return to this screen, and click the Activate button next to the account name. When you do, a dialog box will appear, asking whether you'd like to send the allowance immediately or wait until the first of the next month.

Buy or Redeem Gift Certificates Yes, you can give or cash in iTunes Store gift certificates. To purchase a gift certificate, follow these steps:

1. Click the Buy button in the Buy or Redeem Gift Certificates area.

2. Choose the notification method: Email, Print (which you send or give), or U.S. Mail (which Apple sends).

    If you choose U.S. Mail, iTunes will open your Web browser to a page of the Apple Store where you complete the form.

3. In the next window, choose an amount in denominations ranging from $10 to $200; enter your name as well as the recipient's; and enter any other information that's requested— the recipient's email or snail-mail address, for example.

4. Click Continue.

    You'll be asked to sign into your account one more time to move forward with the transaction.

5. Click Continue in the sign-in window to do so.

    Apple wants to be really sure that you're not just kidding around, so you're asked to confirm your purchase by clicking the Buy button in this last window.

6. Click Buy, and your purchase is recorded.

To redeem any gift certificates sent to you, click the Redeem button. When you do, iTunes' main window will be taken up with the Redeem an iTunes Gift Certificate screen, where you enter a 12-digit gift certificate code to redeem your Store credit.

note Gift certificates can be redeemed only from the store from which they were issued. A gift certificate purchased at the German iTunes Store cannot be redeemed at the U.S. iTunes Store, for example.

iTunes Music Cards

Didn't we just cover that in the Buy & Redeem area? Yes, we did. Apple's stuck it in the Quick Links area separately because some of the people coming to The Store to redeem their iTunes Gift Cards are here for the first time. Apple wanted to make it obvious where to go to redeem these cards.

Support

With this book at your side (or, better yet, open in front of your face), you shouldn't need to click The Store's Support link, but should you come across a problem that's arisen since the publication of this edition, click this link to be taken to Apple's iTunes Store Customer Service Web page. Here, you'll find answers to frequently asked questions about both iTunes and The Store, as well as customer service, billing, and troubleshooting links.

Learn about new music

Wouldn't it be great if someone from The Store called you up to tell whenever Your Very Favorite Artist has a brand-new track ready for download? Recent versions of iTunes offer the next-best thing.

Just click an artist's name to be taken to that artist's page. Glance at the right side of the page, and you'll see the Alert Me link. Click this link, and up pops The Store's sign-in dialog box. Enter your Apple ID and password, click Add, and click OK in the confirmation dialog box; the artist is added to your list of faves. When a new song from this artist becomes available, you'll receive an email alerting you to that fact.

iTunes also includes a feature for recommending music to you based on the music it knows you own. Currently in beta, it's called Just for You. Essentially, iTunes looks at songs you download and recommends music that you're likely to want based on what you already like. (It also gives you the option of identifying music you own that you didn't get from The Store.) Mostly, it's a hit-and-miss idea. I've received some great recommendations and some that are not so great. You can turn the feature on and off via a Just for You link at the bottom of The Store's main page.

Get the Goods

Now that you have an account and can find your way around The Store, it's time to stop manhandling the merchandise and actually buy something. You'll be amazed by how easy (and addictive) this can be.

The pick-and-pay method

The pick-and-pay method is akin to going to a record store, picking up a CD, taking it to the counter, purchasing the disc, returning to the store to pick another CD, purchasing it, going back to the store once again, and ... well, you get the idea. You pay as you go. This is how The Store operates by default. Pick-and-pay works this way:

1. Pick your Poison (or Prince, "Prison Break," or *Pirates of the Caribbean*).

   Using any of the methods I suggested earlier, locate music, audiobooks, or video that you desperately need to own.

2. Click the Buy button.

   To purchase a song or TV episode, click the Buy Song or Buy Episode entry in the Price column that appears in iTunes' main window. To purchase an album, TV season, movie, or audiobook, look near the top of the window for a Buy button. The price of your purchase is listed next to each of these buttons.

At times, you can't download an entire album. Instead, The Store may list a partial album—one from which you can purchase only individual songs. Other times, you can't buy certain music tracks individually; you must purchase the entire album.

3. Enter your Apple ID or AOL screen name and password in the resulting window.

4. Click the Buy button.

   Just to make sure you weren't kidding around when you clicked the Buy button, a new window asks you to confirm your intention to make your purchase. Should you care to banish this window forevermore, check the Don't Warn Me Again check box.

   If you've decided not to purchase the item, click Cancel and go on with your life.

5. Click the Buy button again.

   The media you purchased begins downloading, and you're charged for your purchases. As each item downloads, its progress is monitored in the Downloads folder in iTunes' Source list. You can pause some downloads to give priority to others—pause your podcasts from download-ing to get a TV show or movie more quickly, for example.

The shopping-cart method

If you intend to bulk up your media library significantly in a single shopping session, you may find the pick-and-pay method tedious. The Store offers an alternative—piling all your music into a single shopping cart and checking out in one fell swoop. To do so, follow these steps:

1. Choose iTunes > Preferences on your Mac or Edit > Preferences on your PC.

2. Click the Store icon in the resulting window.

3. Select the Buy Using a Shopping Cart option.

4. Click OK to dismiss the window.

   A Shopping Cart entry appears in iTunes' Source list.

5. Whirl around The Store until you find something you want to purchase.

   The buttons formerly labeled Buy now read Add.

6. Click the Add button to add an item to your shopping cart.

7. Repeat steps 5 and 6 until you can shop no more.

8. Click the Shopping Cart entry in the Source list.

   The main iTunes window displays all the items you've piled into your cart. (Items such as albums and TV seasons that contain multiple tracks or episodes will appear with a triangle next to them. Click the triangle to view the content of the item.)

At the bottom of the window, you'll see the total you'll owe if you proceed. This total does not include sales tax (which—yes—you will be charged).

9. Remove any items you don't want by selecting them and then pressing your computer keyboard's Delete key.

10. Click Buy Now to purchase your media.

Within the shopping cart, you can buy songs or albums individually by clicking Buy Song or Buy Album, or buy everything in the cart by clicking the Buy Now button at the bottom of the iTunes window.

Play with Your Purchase

After the purchased music has found a home on your hard drive, you have several ways to put it to work.

Play it

As you may recall, you are allowed to play purchased media on up to five computers. When you play purchased media for the first time, iTunes checks to see whether the computer is authorized to play it. If so, the music, movie, audiobook, or TV show plays back with no problem. If the computer hasn't been authorized, you'll be prompted for your Apple ID or AOL screen name and password. That name and password, along with some information that identifies your computer, are sent to Apple, where that

Mac or PC is counted against your limit of five authorizations.

If you've used up your authorizations on five other computers, you'll be notified that you must deauthorize one of your computers before you're allowed to play the purchased music. Fortunately, deauthorizing a computer is as simple as choosing Store > Deauthorize Computer in iTunes. When you choose this command, your computer connects to the Internet, and Apple's database is updated to reflect the deauthorization of that particular computer.

After you deauthorize a computer, of course, you can't use it to play back purchased media until you authorize it again. (Yes, this means that if you own more than five computers and intend to play purchased media on all of them, you're going to spend some time playing the deauthorization shuffle.)

note Reformatting the computer's hard drive (or replacing that hard drive) does not deauthorize the machine. Before passing your computer along to someone else, be sure to deauthorize it.

Burn it

People play music on all kinds of devices and in all kinds of environments—on computers, boom boxes, home stereos, and portable music players, and in cars, boats, and planes. (I've even seen a system that allows you to play music in your hot tub.) Forcing you to listen to music only on your computer is silly. And because Apple Computer is anything but silly, it made sure that you'd be able to take your purchased music with you on something other than an iPod, MacBook, or Windows PC. It does so by allowing you to burn purchased music to CD.

When you do so, the .m4p files are converted to red-book audio files—the file format used by commercial audio CDs. These CDs are not copy-protected in any way and behave just like regular ol' audio CDs. Pop 'em into a standard CD player and press Play, and out comes the music.

As I indicated earlier in this chapter, burning your music to CD involves a few limitations. You can burn up to seven copies of a particular playlist. If you attempt to burn an eighth copy, you'll be told that you can't. If you alter that playlist after the seventh burn—by adding or removing a song—you can burn another seven copies. Alter that playlist, and you get seven more copies.

To burn media to disc, create a playlist that contains the media you'd like to record to the disc. At the bottom of the playlist, you'll see a Burn Disc button. Insert a blank CD or DVD and click this button to burn the contents of the playlist onto the disc.

If the contents of the playlist is music only, you'll burn an audio CD. If you're attempting to burn video, that's a different story. iTunes doesn't allow you to burn video—TV shows, music videos, and movies—to discs that can be played on commercial players (such as the DVD player in your living room). Instead, iTunes lets you burn video only as data for the purposes of backup.

Book Burning

Unless the narrator of your purchased audio novel or work of nonfiction reads very quickly, the play time for your purchase is likely to be measured in hours. Yet a recordable CD can store only about 80 minutes of audio. How do you cram all that narration onto a single CD?

You can't. When iTunes burns a book to disc, it converts the file to the file format required by audio CDs—a format that consumes 10 MB of hard disk space per minute of stereo audio.

Fortunately, iTunes provides an easy way to record your audio-books to disc. When you select a file that will exceed the recording capacity of an audio CD and ask iTunes to burn a disc, the program offers to split the file into lengths that can fit on a CD. (If you must know, each segment is 1 hour, 19 minutes, and 56 seconds.) When iTunes fills one CD, it spits it out and asks for another blank disc. It continues to spit and ask until it finishes burning the entire file to disc.

The resulting discs won't be named in an intuitive way—"War and Peace" I, II, and III, for example. Rather, each will simply read "Audio CD" when you insert it into your Mac or PC. For this reason, you should keep a Sharpie at the ready to label each disc as it emerges from your CD burner.

Limited for Your Protection

With every intention of creating a successful distribution system, Apple has tried to address the desires of both consumers and the music industry. Consumers should be pleased that they're allowed to play music purchased at The Store on a variety of devices: computer; portable music player (the iPod); and any commercial CD player, including the ones in your home stereo, boom box, and car. And the music industry's fears of rampant piracy should be calmed because consumers can play that music on a limited number of computers; purchased music files are linked to the person who purchased them; only so many copies of a particular playlist can be burned to CD; and by default, the only music player that can play that music is the iPod.

Following are the specific restrictions Apple imposes on purchased music:

- Purchased music is encoded in a protected version of Dolby Laboratories' Advanced Audio Coding (AAC) format, which bears the .m4p extension (versus the .m4a extension of the standard AAC files that iTunes 4 can create). These files are encoded in a way that makes pirating difficult.

- You may play purchased music on up to five computers, which can be a mix of Macs and Windows PCs. All these computers must be authorized by Apple. If you attempt to play purchased music on an unauthorized computer, you'll be instructed to register the computer online before you can play the music. I describe the ins and outs of authorization in "Play it" earlier in this chapter.

- You may burn up to seven CD copies of a particular playlist that contains purchased music. When you change that playlist—add or subtract a song, for example—you may burn another seven copies. Change the playlist again for another seven burns.

continues on next page

- You cannot burn purchased music on CDs formatted as MP3 discs.

- The name and Apple ID of the person who purchased the music are embedded in each purchased song. Apple does this to discourage buyers from making those songs widely available on the Web (and to trace songs to the rightful owner, should they find their way to the Web).

- Officially, you can download purchased music only one time. In the past, if you lost your music—because your hard drive crashed, for example—you had to purchase it again. Of course you should back up your purchases but in case you don't, Apple has a secret case-by-case policy whereby you may re-download your purchased media one time per year. Contact iTunes Support at www.apple.com/support/itunes/store/lostmusic/#form if you've been thus afflicted.

- All purchases are final. If you download Highway 9's "Heroine," thinking that it's the Velvet Underground's "Heroin," you're stuck with it.

- You can play purchased music on as many iPods as you like, as long as those iPods are running iPod Software 1.3 Updater or later. Earlier versions of the iPod software won't recognize AAC-encoded music (either standard AAC encoding or the protected AAC format used for purchased music).

- You can't burn video to a disc that can be played in a commercial player. Burned videos are for backup purposes only.

5

The Informational iPod

By now, you probably realize that the iPod is the world's greatest portable music player (and a pretty fair video player too!). But take a quick scroll through the Extras screen of any display-bearing iPod, and you'll get the idea that the iPod is more than a music player. Here, you'll find the Contacts, Calendar, and Notes entries, which hint that your iPod is ready to offer up a phone number, remind you of an upcoming appointment, or recall your Aunt Vilma's recipe for Swedish meatballs. Though no substitute for a Palm device (or many of today's mobile phones), the iPod can perform a reasonably convincing impression of a personal information manager. In these pages, I'll show you how to take best advantage of these features by composing, moving, and synchronizing your contacts, calendars, and notes with your iPod.

Make iContact

The first informational feature to appear on early iPods was Contacts. Here's how they work.

Viva vCard

I don't mean to geek you out with technical jargon, but to understand how the iPod works its contact magic, it's helpful to know that, like your computer, the iPod supports something called the *vCard standard*. This is a scheme concocted a couple of decades ago that allows contact files to be read and created on a variety of devices—a computer, mobile phone, or Palm device, for example. The idea is that I can create a contact with my Mac's copy of Address Book and email it to my sister who uses a Windows PC, and she can view that contact in her copy of Microsoft Outlook.

Apple designed the iPod so it also supports vCards. Just plunk a vCard into the right folder on your iPod, and when you next click your iPod's Contacts entry, the rich details of that person, place, or thing will be revealed. The iPod can display the following items:

- **Contact's picture**—an image of the contact (5G iPods only)

- **Contact's formatted name**—Bubba Jones, for example

- **Contact's name**—the name as it appears in the contact (Jones, Bubba, or Dr., for example)

- **Contact's address(es)**—the address types supported by vCard (business, home, mailing, and parcel)

- **Contact's telephone number(s)**—the phone numbers supported by vCard

- **Contact's email**—the email addresses in the contact

- **Contact's title**—Dr., Ms, Mr., and so on

- **Contact's organization**—the company name displayed in the contact

- **Contact's URL**—the Internet address contained in the contact

- **Contact's note**—the note field in the contact

vCard support wouldn't mean much if common applications didn't support it. Fortunately, the universal nature of the standard means that most information- management and email applications you're likely to run across support vCard. As this book goes to press, vCard support is present on the Mac in OS X's Address Book, QUALCOMM's Eudora, Bare Bones Software's Mailsmith, Microsoft's Entourage email clients, and Palm's Palm Desktop 4.x and Now Software's Contact information managers. For Windows, you'll find vCard supported in such main-stays as Windows' Address Book, Microsoft Outlook, and Palm Desktop.

Work with contacts

Now that you understand the underlying structure of the iPod's contacts, you're ready to put them to practical use. In the following pages, you'll create contacts in various applications and export them to the iPod.

The manual method: Macintosh

Much like their paper counterparts, vCards are amenable to being dropped where they can be most helpful. In the case of vCards, this means that you can drag them from their host application (Mac OS X's Address Book application or Microsoft Entourage) onto your Mac's Desktop or into another vCard-friendly application.

Wouldn't it be swell if you could drop them into your iPod just as easily?

You can. Here's how, using Apple's Address Book:

1. Open Address Book.

   You'll find it in Mac OS X's Applications folder at the root level of your startup drive. All the contacts appear in the main window.

2. Select contacts (by pressing Command-A to select all contacts or Command-clicking individual contacts) and drag the selected contacts to the Desktop to create a single vCard file that contains multiple contacts.

Alternatively, you can select your contacts and choose File > Export vCard. The selected contacts will be placed in a single vCard.

3. If your iPod's not connected to your Mac, make the connection, and wait for its icon to appear on the Desktop.

4. Configure your iPod so that it mounts on the Mac's Desktop as an external hard drive (by enabling the Enable Disk Use option in the iPod Preferences window's Summary pane).

5. Double-click the iPod icon on the Desktop to open the iPod's hard drive, where you'll see a Contacts folder.

6. Drag your vCard files into the iPod's Contacts folder (**Figure 5.1**).

Figure 5.1
Copying a vCard file to the iPod's Contacts folder.

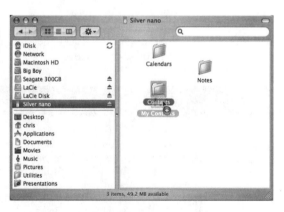

7. Disconnect your iPod, and navigate to the Contacts screen to view your contacts.

The manual method: Windows

Moving contacts manually from Windows applications to the iPod isn't terribly different from performing the operation on the Mac. Here's how to go about it with Windows' Address Book:

1. Launch Address Book.

2. If it's not already selected, choose Main Identity's Contacts in the Address Book window's left pane.

3. Press Ctrl+A to select all the contacts, or hold down the Ctrl key while clicking noncontiguous contacts to select multiple contacts individually.

4. Drag the contacts to the desktop.

5. Mount your iPod, and open it by double-clicking its icon in the My Computer window.

6. Drag your contacts into the iPod's Contacts folder.

Your contacts have been moved to the iPod as individual vCard files.

Sort Your Contacts

The iPod is just the tiniest bit flexible in how it lets you view your contacts. It lets you choose independently to sort and view them alphabetically, first or last name first. To set your contact sorting and display preferences, highlight the Settings entry in the iPod's main screen, press the Center button, and scroll down to Contacts. Press the Center button again, and you'll find the Sort and Display options. Each option allows you to select First and Last or Last and First, thus allowing you to sort by last name but display your contacts' first name first and last name . . . well, last.

7. Unmount your iPod by clicking the iPod icon in the system tray and choosing Unmount from the resulting contextual menu.

8. Wait for the iPod to reboot; then navigate to the Contacts screen.

The contacts you copied are displayed in the Contacts list.

The process I've just outlined is fairly common across applications. Whether you're using Palm Desktop, Microsoft's Entourage or Outlook, or some other email client or contact manager, you'll likely find a way to drag contacts from the program to the desktop as vCards and/or locate an Export command somewhere in the program's File menu that lets you export contacts as vCards.

The nice thing is that it may not be necessary to do any of this dragging and exporting. Beginning with iTunes 5, there's a way for Mac and Windows users to sync their Address Book contacts with their iPods automatically.

The automated method: Macintosh

Once upon a time, a program called iSync was responsible for syncing contacts and calendars with an iPod. No longer. iTunes now offers this feature. Here's how it works:

1. Plug your iPod into your Mac.

2. Select your iPod in iTunes' Source list and then click the Contacts tab.

3. Enable the Sync Address Book Contacts option.

To place all the contacts in Address Book on your iPod, make sure that the All Contacts option is enabled. If you'd rather place only certain contacts on the iPod, enable the Selected Groups Only option, and in the list below, choose the groups whose contacts you'd like to copy to the iPod (**Figure 5.2**). You may want only your business contacts or friends and family contacts on your iPod, for example. Grouping those contacts in Address Book and then selecting those groups in iTunes is the way to do it.

Figure 5.2
The Contacts pane in the Macintosh version of iTunes 7.

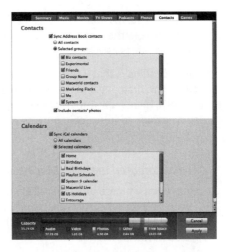

If you plug a 5G iPod into your Mac, you'll see an option to copy your contacts' pictures to the iPod.

4. Click the Apply button at the bottom of the pane.

iTunes will synchronize the selected contacts between your Mac and the iPod.

The automated method: Windows

With iTunes 5, Apple finally brought contact and calendar synchronization to the Windows version of the program. iTunes for Windows will synchronize Windows' Address Book and Outlook contacts and calendars with your iPod. To make it do so, you follow a procedure similar to the one I outlined for the Macintosh.

Fire up iTunes with your iPod connected, select your iPod in iTunes' Source list, and click the Contacts tab. Within this pane, you can elect to synchronize contacts from Windows Address Book or Outlook. And as with the Macintosh version of iTunes, you can choose to synchronize all contacts or just selected groups. If you choose Outlook, it will launch automatically.

Remove contacts from your iPod

So you've broken up with your boyfriend, your favorite dry cleaner has gone out of business, or you can't recall who this "Jane" person is? There's no need to pack your iPod with contacts you don't need; you can remove them easily. Here's how:

1. If your iPod's not connected to your computer, make the connection, and wait for its icon to appear on the Mac's Desktop or in Windows' My Computer window.

2. Configure your iPod so that it mounts on the computer as an external hard drive.

3. Double-click the iPod icon to open the iPod's hard drive.

4. Locate and open the Contacts folder on this hard drive.

5. Select the contacts you'd like to remove, and drag them to the Trash on the Mac or the Recycle Bin on the PC.

6. Disconnect your iPod by dragging its icon to the Trash on the Mac or by unmounting it in Windows' system tray.

tip

On a Mac, if the contact you want to remove is part of a single vCard file that contains multiple names, just remove the contact from Address Book and resync the iPod. The contact will be gone. (Outlook doesn't support vCards that hold multiple contacts.)

I Need Contact!

If, like many Mac users, you've carefully squirreled away your contacts in Microsoft's Entourage or Palm's Palm Desktop, you may be disappointed that iTunes works only with Address Book. But as Cicero was so fond of saying, "It's no use crying over spilled goat's milk."

If you want to use iTunes and don't care to pay for a third-party utility, you must use Address Book. Fortunately, it's not difficult to move contacts from Entourage or Palm Desktop into Address Book. Here's how:

ENTOURAGE

1. In Mac OS X 10.2 or earlier, open the AppleScript folder inside Mac OS X's Applications folder, and double-click the Script Menu.menu item. In Mac OS X 10.3 and later, double-click the Install Script Menu application in this same location.

This places an AppleScript menu in the Mac's menu bar.

2. Choose AppleScript > Mail Scripts; then choose the Import Addresses script from the submenu.

When you run this script, a window appears that gives you the option to import addresses from Entourage, Outlook Express, Palm Desktop, Eudora, Claris Emailer, or Netscape into Mac OS X's Address Book.

3. Choose Entourage, and click OK.

The script will run and copy your Entourage addresses to Mac OS X's Address Book.

continues on next page

PALM DESKTOP (VERSION 4 AND LATER)

You can also move Palm Desktop contacts to Address Book with the script I just described, but if you'd like to try a different method, follow these steps:

1. Launch Palm Desktop, and choose Window > Address List.

2. In the resulting Address List window, select the contacts you'd like to move to OS X's Address Book.

3. Choose File > Export.

4. In the resulting Export: Palm Desktop window, name your file, select the Desktop as the destination for your saved file, and choose vCard from the Format pop-up menu.

5. Click the Export button.

A vCard containing all the selected contacts is saved to the Desktop.

6. Open Address Book, and drag the vCard into either the Group or Name portion of the window.

In a flash, your contacts appear in Address Book, ready for exporting to your iPod via iTunes.

OLDER CONTACT MANAGERS

Those who use older contact managers, such as TouchBase and DynoDex, may believe that they've been left out of the party. Not so. Although these contact managers won't run in Mac OS X (or, likely, in Mac OS 9), you can still pull their data into Address Book. The means for doing so is Palm Desktop.

Palm Desktop began life as Claris Organizer, and it retains the file compatibility that it had in its Claris incarnation. Just use Palm Desktop's Import command to open your old contact-manager file (you may need to move a few fields around during the import process to make the data line up correctly) and then export it as a vCard file.

Make a Date

As I explained earlier in the chapter, contacts and the iPod carry on their cozy relationship thanks to the vCard standard. Another couple of standards, called the *vCal* and *iCalendar* standards, help the iPod understand *calendar events*. These are universal formats for exchanging calendar and scheduling information between vCal- and iCalendar-aware applications and devices.

When you add a calendar event to your iPod, the following information will appear in the Event screen:

- **The date of the appointment.** The date is displayed in day/month/year format—11 Jan 2007, for example.

- **The time and duration of the appointment.** This info is displayed as 4:00–5:30 PM, for example.

- **The name of the appointment.** If you've named it My Appointment in your computer's calendar application, so shall it be named on your iPod.

- **The attendees.** If you've added attendees to the appointment in your computer's calendar application, those names will appear next in the Event screen.

- **Notes.** Any notes you've entered on your computer will appear last in the Event screen.

note Visible and audible alarms are also transferred to your iPod. But you'll see no indication in the Event screen—or anywhere else, for that matter—that such alarms exist (though you'll have a pretty good idea when the alarm goes off).

Work with calendars

Apple would have looked mighty foolish adding
calendaring capabilities to the iPod without also
providing Mac users a calendar application. It did so
by releasing iCal, a free, basic calendar application
that runs under Mac OS X 10.2 and later.

If you have a Mac that's incapable of running the
last couple of iterations of Mac OS X, fear not; iCal
isn't the only Macintosh application that's compatible with the iPod. Both Microsoft Entourage (part
of Microsoft Office X and Microsoft Office 2004 for
Macintosh) and Palm's Palm Desktop 4.x can also
export iPod-compatible vCal files.

Windows users can create iPod-friendly calendar
files, too; unfortunately, they can't do it with an
Apple application. Although iCal and the Windows
iPod were announced in nearly the same breath,
Apple didn't feel compelled to release a version of
iCal for Windows. Fortunately, Windows users who
have a copy of Microsoft Office will discover that
Outlook can export calendar files that are compatible with the iPod, as can Palm's Palm Desktop 4.x.

The following sections show you how to make the
most of calendars with your computer's common
calendar applications.

iCal (Mac OS X 10.2 or later)

Although you can move iCal calendars into your
iPod by selecting a calendar in iCal, choosing File >
Export, and dragging the resulting calendar file into

the iPod's Calendars folder, why bother when iTunes provides a more expedient method? To use iTunes, just follow these steps:

1. Plug your iPod into your Mac.

2. Select your iPod, and click the Contacts tab.

   iPod veterans may recall that iPod Preferences used to have both Contacts and Calendars panes. In iTunes 7, Apple combined those functions into a single Contacts pane.

3. Enable the Sync iCal Calendars option.

   This is sounding familiar, right? Yes, it's very much like moving contacts via iTunes. Similarly, you can choose to synchronize All Calendars or Selected Calendars. When you choose the latter option, just check the boxes next to the calendars you want to copy to the iPod, and click OK.

4. Click the Apply button.

   iTunes will synchronize the selected calendars between your Mac and the iPod.

Outlook (Windows)

You guessed it—syncing calendars on a Windows PC is darned similar to doing it on the Mac. The major difference is that there is no iCal for Windows. Instead, you have the option to synchronize all your Outlook calendars or just selected calendars.

View events

To view the appointments for a particular day on your iPod, scroll to that date on the iPod's calendar, and press the Center button. In the next screen, a list of appointments for that day appears. Scroll to the appointment you want to view, and press the Center button again. The details of that appointment are displayed in the iPod's Event screen.

Notes-worthy Feature

If you select Notes from the Extras screen on a Dock-connector iPod (notes aren't supported on earlier iPods or, obviously, the screenless iPod shuffle) and then select the Instructions entry, you'll learn that you can view plain-text notes on your iPod. But there's more to know about Notes than that:

- **Notes are strictly limited to 4 Kbits.** If a note exceeds 4 Kbits, the excess text is cut off.

- **The iPod can hold up to 1,000 notes.** If the iPod's Notes folder contains more than 1,000 notes, only the first 1,000 notes are displayed. (The first 1,000 are determined by alphabetical order rather than creation date.)

- **Notes are cached in memory.** After you've viewed a note, its contents are stored in a 64 KB memory cache. This cache is useful because it allows the iPod to display the note without spinning up the hard drive, thereby extending the battery charge. When the cache overflows (because you've read

more than 64 KB of data into it), the oldest notes
are given the boot to make room for the information being copied into the cache.

- **Notes support a very basic set of HTML tags** (the
  Hypertext Markup Language codes used to create
  Web pages). These tags allow you to create notes
  that link to other notes or to songs on your iPod.

You may be thinking, "Well, ain't this ducky, Chris, but
other than providing a place to store directions to
Auntie Di's suburban manse or the French transla-
tion of 'I'm sorry, but this éclair appears to be stuffed
with haddock,' what earthly use are these notes?"

Notes can be linked via the HTML tags I mentioned
earlier, which opens a host of possibilities. Museums,
for example, can use notes that are linked to one
another (and to the iPod's audio tracks) to create
audio guides, with notes that link to audio descrip-
tions of paintings in a particular gallery. And real
estate agents can offer potential buyers iPod-led
tours of new properties.

Creating linked notes isn't rocket science, but regrettably, I can't describe all its ins and outs in this short
guide. If you'd like more details, check out the latest
edition of my vastly more detailed *Secrets of the iPod
and iTunes*, also from Peachpit Press.

6

Accessories

At one time, nearly everything you needed for a happy iPodding experience came in the box: the iPod; a power adapter; the right cables; a case; a remote control; a Dock; and, of course, the software necessary to make it all work. That's changed. As Apple has lowered iPod prices while offering models with equal or higher capacities, it's determined to protect its profit by making once-bundled accessories pay-for options.

At the risk of verging onto the editorial, I don't think that's such a bad thing. Though it was nice enough to get a "free" case and remote control, I quickly threw them into the iPod Extras box that sits next to my desk and replaced them with accessories that suit my tastes. It bothers me not one bit to take the $100 that I saved from the iPod's previous price and devote that money to the accessories I want.

Looking upon the dearth of accessories bundled with today's iPods as an opportunity rather than a punishment, let's examine the kinds of items that will enhance your iPod.

Down to Cases

If you carry around an unprotected iPod or iPod nano, it won't be long before you notice the effect gravity can have on objects dropped from an inverted shirt pocket—or what a pants-pocketful of loose change and keys can do to an iPod's surface. Your iPod needs the protection a good case can provide. And what will such a case provide?

What to look for

A good case should offer the following features:

- A system for attaching the iPod to your body (a belt clip or strap for the iPod; a case, lanyard, or clip for the iPod nano or iPod shuffle)

- Construction sturdy enough to protect the iPod from scratches

- A place to store a full-size iPod's earbuds

These features are the bare minimum you should expect from your case. Frankly, with a piece of bubble wrap, a clothespin, and a couple of pieces of duct tape, you could construct a case that meets these requirements. Looking beyond the essentials, what else might you look for?

- A way to detach the iPod from your body easily

  At times, you'll want to fiddle with the iPod—adjust the volume, flick on the Hold switch, or use the controls to skip a song. Look for a clip that releases quickly and effortlessly.

- A way to access the controls easily

  A standard iPod or iPod nano case that opens in the front lets you fiddle with the controls. You should also be able to access the Headphone jack—and, ideally, the Dock Connector port and Hold switch—without having to disassemble the case.

- Design sturdy enough to provide your iPod a reasonable chance of survival, should you drop it

- Design that makes a statement

  Let's face it—you dropped a lot of cash on your iPod. The iPod is cool. It deserves a cool case.

On the cases

As this book goes to print, there are exactly 1 jillion iPod cases, and there's no way I can cover them all in this small book. Rather than recommend count-less cases, as I do in *Secrets of the iPod and iTunes*, I'll discuss the case styles you're likely to run across and a few standout examples of each kind. Many case

designs are available in different sizes (with varia-
tions in price) for full-size iPods, minis, and nanos.
Unless otherwise noted, prices quoted here are for
standard iPod-sized cases; all are subject to change.

Hard-shell cases

Many iPod cases are designed primarily for protection. Oh, sure, they may be as fashionable as can
be, but in addition to having a pretty face, each
understands that its mission is to keep your iPod
from exploding into a passel of parts should you
drop it. Some of these cases can be on the bulky
side. Marware's (www.marware.com) $35 Sportsuit
Convertible case, for example, offers great protection, and it's good looking, but it won't slip easily into
your inside jacket pocket (**FIGURE 6.1**). Others—such
as Contour Design's (www.contourcase.com) $33
Showcase Video, Matias' (http://matias.ca) $40
Armor for iPod, and Vaja's (www.vajacases.com) $70
i-volution—are attractive cases that are a little less
bulky but still pack a load of protection.

Figure 6.1
Marware's
Sportsuit
Convertible
case.

Sports cases

Although you can subject hard-shell cases to a load of abuse, if you intend to expose your iPod to hostile environments—particularly those that are more than a little moist—seek a sports case. Cases such as OtterBox's (www.otterbox.com) $50 OtterBox for iPod Video and H2O Audio's (www.h2oaudio.com) $90 H2O Audio for iPod (with Video) cases are waterproof up to about 3 to 10 feet.

Soft-shell cases

Despite the classification I've slapped on these things, soft-shell cases can also keep your iPod safe from harm. Of these cases, I'm very keen on Waterfield Designs' (www.sfbags.com) $29 iPod Video Case (which fits all full-size iPods). It's nicely constructed and offers good protection, and I find its black ballistic nylon with colored piping attractive. Waterfield also makes two woman's-clutch-purse-like iPod Gear Pouches for carrying a slew of iPod gear—$29 for the small pouch (for your nano) and $35 for the larger pouch.

Skins and sleeves

If all you're looking for is protection from scratches, a skin or sleeve for your iPod may be enough. (It's not enough for me, but then again, I'm the cautious sort.) I don't have any particular skins or sleeves to recommend, so I'll leave it up to you to pick one that lights up your life.

I will, however, suggest that regardless of which display-bearing iPod you have, you look into Power Support's (www.powersupportusa.com) Crystal Film cover sets. These are scratch-resistant transparent films that you apply to the face and back of your iPod. They won't protect your iPod from bumps and bruises, but they will guard it from scratches. Best of all, they're held on by static cling; no adhesives will mar your iPod when you take them off. They run $15 for the nano and $16 for full-size iPods.

Adaptive Technology

Although the iPod's Headphone jack is labeled with the headphones symbol, that jack can accommodate more than just the iPod's earbuds. The iPod's Headphone jack can send out perfectly clean audio from this port to your computer's sound input port or to a home or car stereo. All you need to perform this feat is the right cable. I'll show you exactly which cables to use and how to string them properly from the iPod or Dock to the device of your choice.

iPod to computer

If you want to record directly from your iPod to your computer's audio port, you need an adapter cable that carries stereo Walkman-style miniplugs on both ends. (You can distinguish a stereo miniplug from the mono variety by the two black bands on the plug. A mono miniplug has just one black band.)

You can find such cables at your local electronics boutique for less than $5 for a 6-foot cable. Higher-quality cables that include better shielding, thicker cable, and gold connectors can cost significantly more.

iPod to home stereo

Take the *personal* out of *personal music player* by attaching your iPod or Dock to your home stereo and subjecting the rest of the household to your musical whims. You need nothing more than a cable that features a stereo miniplug on one end and two mono RCA plugs on the other. A cheap version of this cable costs less than $5.

Plug the miniplug into the iPod's or Dock's audio jack and the two RCA plugs into an input on your stereo receiver (the AUX input, for example). With this arrangement, you can control the volume not only with your stereo's volume control, but also (if the cable is connected to the Headphone port) with the iPod's scroll wheel.

iPod to two headphones

There may (and I hope there *will*) come a time when you'll want to snuggle up with your snookums and listen to your Special Song played on an iPod. A touch of romance goes out of this ritual, however, when you have to split a pair of earbuds between your li'l sweet potato and you.

To bring the intimacy back to your musical relation-ship, purchase a stereo line splitter. Such an adapter bears a single stereo male miniplug connector on one end (the end you plug into the iPod) and two stereo female miniplug connectors on the other. Plug a pair of headphones into each female connector, and you're set. SmartShare, a $15 headphone splitter from Griffin Technology (www.griffintechnology.com), sports separate volume controls for each output.

iPod to car stereo

This one's a bit trickier. Increasingly, car stereos include an iPod Dock connector or miniplug jacks for plugging devices such as your iPod into the car's sound system. If you have such a connector or jack, you're in luck. Just use the appropriate cable, and you're ready to rock. If you don't have a connector, a technician at a Ye Olde Auto Stereo Shoppe may be able to provide one by tapping into a hidden connector on the back of the car stereo. (That same technician may be able to recommend an in-car iPod system that won't cost you an arm and a leg.) If taking your car to such a tech sounds like a bother (or just too expensive), you have two other options: a cassette-player adapter or an FM transmitter.

Cassette-player adapter

If your car has a cassette player, you can use a cassette adapter. This thing looks exactly like an audiocassette, save for the thin cable that trails from the back edge. To use one of these adapters, shove it into your car's cassette player, plug its cable into your iPod, and press the Play buttons on both the iPod and the cassette player. Music should issue from your car's speakers.

These adapters cost less than $20. Note, however, that an adapter that works in one cassette player may not work in another. Be sure you can return it for a refund in case your player exhibits an aversion to these doodads.

FM transmitter

These devices work like radio stations, broadcasting whatever is plugged into them to a nearby FM radio. FM transmitters work in a very limited range. Move them more than a dozen feet from the radio's antenna, and you'll pick up interference. For this reason, most are not ideal for use with a home stereo.

Their effectiveness in an automobile depends on how heavily populated the airwaves around you are and how sensitive your car's antenna is. A strong radio signal will overpower these devices, rendering them ineffective. If you live in an urban area with a plethora of active radio stations (or plan to travel in one routinely), you may want to explore a hard-wired connection or a cassette adapter.

When seeking an FM transmitter, find one that can transmit outside the normal FM range—to 97.9, for example. U.S. radio stations are forbidden to broadcast at this frequency, but many car radios can tune it in. If yours does, and your transmitter broadcasts to this frequency, you've got a better chance of getting a clean signal.

Also look for a transmitter that can broadcast in mono, such as the $50 and $70 iTrip transmitters

Figure 6.2
Griffin
Technology's
iTrip nano FM
transmitter.

made by Griffin Technology (**FIGURE 6.2**). Transmitters that do this put out a stronger signal that's more likely to overpower encroaching radio stations. Sure, you lose stereo separation, but at least you're not listening to hiss and static.

Finally, transmitters that plug into your car's cigarette lighter port offer not only the advantage that they provide power to your iPod, but also tend to put out a more powerful signal.

As the capabilities of FM transmitters change fairly frequently, I'll tell you only that these devices are made by companies such as Belkin (www.belkin.com), DLO (www.dlo.com), Griffin Technology, and Kensington (www.kensington.com). I've reviewed many for *Playlist* magazine (www.playlistmag.com); check there for up-to-date evaluations.

Power to the People

Like the heads of government, your iPod needs power to do its job. To bring power to your iPod, consider these accessories.

iPod Power Adapter

Once upon a time, Apple included power adapters with full-size iPods. No more. Because it's a drag to have to find a computer with an available powered USB port (or FireWire port, if you have the right cable) to charge your iPod, I think an iPod Power Adapter is a necessity. Apple will sell you one for $29.

PocketDock

When you're living the iPod lifestyle, it's practically inevitable: You need to charge or sync your iPod, but its cable is in another zip code, and you wish you could use a standard USB or FireWire cable to plug it into your laptop or a friend's PC. PocketDock adapters from SendStation (www.sendstation.com) grant that wish—and can make it easier to plug your iPod into a stereo, as well.

There are four versions of the PocketDock, all just bigger than a quarter and ready to attach to your key ring. Each has one of Apple's proprietary male data/power Dock connectors on one end and a USB and/or FireWire connector on the other.

The $30 PocketDock with Line Out USB (**Figure 6.3**) features a USB 2.0 connector plus an audio line-out port for a stereo miniplug; it even comes with a 6-foot mini-to-dual RCA connector cable you can plug into an amp.

Figure 6.3
SendStation's
PocketDock
with Line Out
USB.

The $30 PocketDock with Line Out FireWire sports the same audio port but a FireWire connector instead of USB. The $23 PocketDock Combo features both USB 2.0 and FireWire connectors, sans audio port. The $15 PocketDock FireWire, originally designed to let Dock-connector iPods work with pre-Dock-connector accessories, offers a FireWire connector only. (Note that FireWire-only PocketDocks can charge, but not sync, 5G iPods and iPod nanos.)

World Travel Adapter Kit

The iPod can automatically accommodate the world's two major power standards: 115 and 230 volts. The iPod Power Adapter, however, comes with just one plug—of whatever type is used in the country where it was sold. If you plan to take your iPod globe-trotting, you'll need the proper plug adapter. Apple's $39 World Travel Adapter Kit contains plug adapters for outlets in North America, Japan, China, the United Kingdom, continental Europe, Korea, Australia, and Hong Kong.

Auto charger

To keep your iPod topped off on the road, you need an auto charger. The device plugs into your car's ciga-rette lighter or 12-volt receptacle; it delivers power to your iPod through a plug that fits into the iPod's Dock connector port. There are lots of these char-gers on the market. I prefer Griffin Technology's $20 PowerJolt because it includes a detachable cable you can use as a spare for syncing your iPod.

Backup batteries

Fat lot of good a power adapter and auto charger do you if you're flying halfway around the world or traipsing through one of the less-welcoming Costa Rican jungles during the latest Eco-Challenge. If you plan to be removed from a ready source of power for a period longer than the typical life of an iPod charge, you need some extra help.

Currently, a few companies offer that help. If you want a battery that refuses to die (and you're willing to put up with a little bulk to get it) ,take a gander at Battery Geek's (www.batterygeek.net) $70 GeekPod 100. It's an external lithium-ion battery, about the size of your iPod, that plugs into the Dock connector and provides more than 100 hours of extra music playback.

For something a bit smaller, try Griffin Technology's $20 TuneJuice, a small adapter powered by a 9-volt battery that will provide you an extra 8 hours of music playback time per battery.

The Ears Have It

The iPod's earbuds are perfectly serviceable. But this style of headphone is inherently problematic, because (a) not all ear canals are the same size, so a set of one-size-fits-all earbuds may not fit all, and (b) some people get the heebie-jeebies when items are lodged inside their ears. For these reasons, your list of accessories may include an additional set of headphones. Headphones come in a variety of styles—including earbuds, neckband, open-air, and closed—from such companies as Etymotic, Shure, Sony, Koss, Aiwa, Panasonic, Philips, and Sennheiser.

Earbuds

If you like earbud-style headphones but find those
included with the iPod to be uncomfortable (particularly if you have the original earbuds, which many
users thought were too big), earbuds are available
from a variety of manufacturers. Look for earbuds
that fit well, don't require a lot of fiddling to focus
(meaning that you don't have to move them around
continually to make them sound good), and offer
reasonably well-balanced sound.

Neckband headphones

These popular headphones are secured to your head
with wires that drape over the tops of your ears.
Imagine putting on a pair of tight glasses backward,
so that the lenses are on the back of your head,
and you'll get the idea. Neckband headphones are
comfortable but easy to dislodge if you tug on the
cable. Also, they don't provide a lot of sound isolation, which means that sounds from outside tend to
filter through.

Open-air headphones

Open-air headphones sit over the ears without
enclosing them completely. When you bought
your portable CD player, open-air headphones likely
were included in the box. These headphones are
comfortable, but the less-expensive models can
sound thin. Like neckband headphones, they don't
provide much isolation.

Closed headphones

Closed headphones cover your ears completely and provide a lot of isolation, leaving you undistracted by outside sounds and those around you undisturbed by a lot of sound bleeding out of your headphones. Some closed headphones can be a bit bulky and uncomfortable, particularly if you wear glasses, so be sure to try before you buy. And because of their size, these headphones aren't terribly portable.

Miscellanea

And then there are the iPod accessories that defy categorization. If you've done the rest, try these accessories on for size.

iPod microphones

At one time, full-size Dock-connector iPods could record "voice-quality" audio (8 kHz, mono) through a compatible microphone attachment. When Apple released the 5G iPod, it quietly included an unexpected upgrade; these new iPods can record CD-quality audio (44.1 kHz, stereo) with a compatible adapter.

Such adapters include Belkin's $70 TuneTalk Stereo for iPod with Video, Griffin Technology's $50 iTalk Pro, and XtremeMac's (www.xtrememac.com) $60 MicroMemo (**Figure 6.4**). The MicroMemo includes a small speaker, which lets you to listen to your recordings. Each of these devices lets you record through a built-in microphone or attach an external mic via a miniplug input jack.

Figure 6.4
XtremeMac's
MicroMemo
microphone
adapter.

Although these adapters weren't originally designed for it, they will work with a second-generation (2G) nano, which also supports audio recording.

iPod camera connectors

By now, you know that you can add pictures to your color iPod via iTunes. But Apple's $29 iPod Camera Connector lets you download pictures directly from your digital camera to the iPod and then view those pictures on your iPod—no processing by iTunes necessary.

The iPod Camera Connector plugs into the bottom of your color iPod and features a USB port, into which you plug your digital camera cable. Select the Import command that appears on your iPod's screen when you plug in a camera, and push the Center button. Pictures are downloaded from the camera to your iPod, where they can be viewed immediately (unless they're RAW images; the iPod can't display those). This connector works only with full-size color iPods.

iPod Radio Remote

If you spend a lot of time in inhospitable climates with your iPod, you may prefer to keep it in your pocket. In that case, you may be a candidate for Apple's iPod Radio Remote. This $49 wired device jacks into your iPod's Dock Connector port and lets you access the iPod's play controls without removing the device from a case or pocket. And it does more: It also holds a small radio receiver. When you plug it into your iPod, a special Radio screen appears, where you can tune the radio to an FM frequency (no AM, sorry) with the iPod's click wheel. The iPod Radio Remote includes a set of Apple's earbuds. This accessory is compatible only with 5G iPods and the iPod nano.

note The iPod Radio Remote works with slideshows and videos as well as with music tracks.

Wireless remote controls

You can also control your full-size iPod and iPod mini without need of wires, using remote controls made by ABT (www.abtech2.com), Apple, DLO, Engineered Audio (www.engineeredaudio.com), Griffin Technology, and TEN Technology (www.tentechnology. com). These are either IR (infrared) or RF (radio frequency) remotes that allow you to control an iPod from a distance, presumably when it's connected to your home or car stereo. The RF remotes—including ABT's $40 iJet Wireless Remote with Bottom Dock and Griffin's $40 AirClick—allow you to stand farther away from the iPod and can work through walls (IR remotes require line of sight).

Dock

If you have a Dock-connector iPod, and you routinely plant it next to your computer or home stereo, Apple's $39 iPod Universal Dock is worth your consideration. A Dock is particularly useful for those with full-size color iPods, as the Dock includes an S-Video port that allows you to project higher-quality slideshows on an attached television or projector. The Universal Dock also has a sensor for the $39 IR-based Apple Remote control that ships with recent-vintage Macintoshes and MacBooks (but not with the Dock itself). You can use the IR-based Remote with the Dock to play, pause, or skip tracks from across the room.

If you'd like a more expansive dock—one that allows you to control the docked iPod via a full-featured remote control—check out DLO's $100 HomeDock. It includes composite, S-Video, and RCA audio output ports. It also includes a USB port so you can sync the iPod directly from the Dock. For an extra $50, DLO's Home Dock Deluxe lets you navigate your iPod's music menus via a television interface.

The ever-so-simple iPod shuffle lacks a Dock connector (and so cannot be controlled remotely), but it does of course use its own flavor of dock for charging and syncing purposes. If you'd like an extra shuffle dock for use at your office or to tuck in your travel bag, Apple will sell you one for $29.

iPod AV Cable

This is another "Apple used to include it" cable—one that lets you connect your full-size color iPod to a television or projector. The $19 cable features a special miniplug on one end that plugs into the iPod's Headphone jack; the split cable on the other end includes left and right RCA plugs, and a composite video connector for plugging into your TV. Because the iPod nano can't project video to televisions, nano owners can skip this one.

iPod speakers

The best way to share your iPod's music with those around you is to jack it into a set of powered speakers. Thanks to the iPod's phenomenal popularity, you can find iPod-friendly speakers that fit just about every budget and taste.

Generally speaking, these speakers include some variety of Dock connector for plugging in your iPod—though many also include a miniplug input port that allows you to plug in older iPods that don't have Dock Connector ports, as well as other audio devices, such as minidisc players and other portable music players. Altec Lansing's (www.alteclansing.com) inMotion series is a good place to start if you're looking for particularly portable iPod speakers. The $200 iM9 sounds good for a smallish docking speaker system and can be easily transported with the included backpack; the $100 iM4 speakers fold up to the size of a large paperback book and are very easy to carry.

Logitech's (www.logitech.com) $150 mm50 Portable Speakers for iPod are another good choice if you're looking for portable iPod speakers. Available in black or white, the speakers sound good for a small system. They run off AC or battery power, sync and power the iPod via a Dock connector, and include a remote control.

If, like me, you'd like an iPod in every room, Tivoli Audio's (www.tivoliaudio.com) $300 iSongBook is the perfect system for your kitchen (**FIGURE 6.5**). Featuring a fold-out dock on the side of the unit, the iSongBook is not only a portable iPod speaker unit, but also an AM/FM clock radio with remote control. It offers balanced—though not blasting— sound. It's portable enough that you can drag it into the bedroom at night and, thanks to its alarm func- tion, wake to the sound of your favorite playlist in the morning.

Figure 6.5
Tivoli Audio's
iSongBook.

Bose's (www.bose.com) $300 SoundDock features great sound in a single package. It cradles the iPod in a Dock connector backed by a full-face metal grille that hides a pair of speakers a bit larger than those in some competing portable systems, allowing the SoundDock to deliver a richer bass.

For bigger, better, and more expensive speakers, check out Audioengine's (www.audioengineusa.com) $349 Audioengine 5 speakers. Though they lack a Dock connector (you'll need to provide your own Dock or connect your iPod via the included miniplug cable),

Shopping for Headphones

You wouldn't purchase a pair of stereo speakers without listening to them, would you? It's just as important to audition a set of headphones that you intend to spend a lot of time with. When you're auditioning those headphones, keep the following factors in mind:

- **SOUND QUALITY.** A good set of headphones provides a nice balance of highs and lows without emphasizing one band of frequencies over another. Listen for a natural sound. If the headphones lack brightness—or if you can't clearly discern low-frequency instruments (such as bass guitar, cello, or kick drum), and hearing your music clearly matters to you—move on. These aren't the headphones for you.

- **COMFORT AND FIT.** If you're an enthusiastic listener, you may wear those headphones for long stretches of time. If they pinch your ears or head, slip out of your ears, or fall off your head, you'll grow tired of them quickly.

- **SIZE.** If you plan to take your headphones with you, look for a pair that fits easily into a pocket or iPod case.

these amplified bookshelf speakers sound amazing given their size and price. Better yet, the left speaker includes an extra input for plugging in an addition audio device. This, coupled with a power outlet on the back of the speaker, provides an easy way to connect Apple's AirPort Express—a wireless base station that allows you to play iTunes music wirelessly.

7

Tips and Tricks

You're far enough along in this little guide to understand that the iPod and iTunes hold more secrets
than just Rip, Click, and Play. This dynamic duo has
other wonders to behold if you know how to unleash
them. And that's exactly the point of this chapter—
to shed light on the lesser-known marvels of the iPod
and iTunes.

Let the magic begin.

Move Media off the iPod

To deter piracy, iTunes and the iPod were designed so that media would travel in one direction only: from the computer to the iPod. When you double-click an iPod mounted on a computer, you'll find no folder within that holds the device's music or movies. Yet this material has to be there somewhere.

It is. It's invisible.

When Apple designed the iPod's copy-protection scheme, it did so understanding one of the fundamental laws of this new millennium: That which can be locked will be unlocked (by a 12-year-old boy).

Rather than dump millions of dollars into a complicated copy-protection scheme—which would almost immediately be broken by one of those wily 12-year-olds—the company did the wise thing and protected the iPod in such a way that honest folks aren't tempted to pilfer music and movies off another's iPod. The company's engineers did nothing more than make the iPod's Music folder invisible (and yes, movies are stored in the Music folder too). Therefore, the trick to getting the media off the iPod is accessing this invisible folder.

Brute-force techniques

Though fairly graceless, one of the easiest ways to retrieve your media from an iPod is to make the iPod's Music folder visible and drag it over to your computer's desktop. Then simply add that folder (and the music within) to iTunes by dragging the folder into iTunes' main window or by choosing File > Add to Library in iTunes. Here's how to do this on either a Mac or a Windows PC.

Macintosh

The Mac doesn't include a utility for making invisible files visible, so you must download one. My favorite tool for this job is Marcel Bresink's free TinkerTool (www.bresink.de/osx/TinkerTool.html). After you've downloaded TinkerTool, follow these steps:

1. Plug in the iPod.

2. If iTunes doesn't launch automatically, launch it.

   If the library on your iPod is not linked to iTunes' library (as would be the case when you're restoring your library from your iPod to a reformatted drive with a freshly installed copy of iTunes), iTunes will ask if you'd like to replace the contents of the iPod with the contents of the iTunes Library. Answer No.

3. Select the iPod in iTunes' Source list; enable the Manually Manage Music and Videos option and the Enable Disk Use option in the resulting Summary pane; then click Apply.

4. Launch TinkerTool, and click the Finder tab.

5. Enable the Show Hidden and System Files option.

6. Click Relaunch Finder.

7. Move to the Finder, and double-click the iPod's icon on the Desktop.

Figure 7.1 The once-invisible iPod_Control folder.

iPod_Control

You'll discover that several more items now appear in the iPod window. Among them is a folder called iPod_Control (**Figure 7.1**).

8. Double-click the iPod_Control folder.

Inside the iPod_Control folder, you'll find the Device, iTunes, and Music folders, along with some other files.

9. Drag the Music folder to the Desktop to copy it to your computer.

As the name does *not* imply, it's also where movies, videos, and other media are kept.

In earlier versions of iTunes, you could simply drag this Music folder to iTunes' main window, and the music within it would be copied to iTunes' music library. This is no longer the case. Now you must flip the visibility bit of this folder (and the folders within it) to copy the files to the library.

10. Use SkyTag Software's $40 File Buddy 8 (www.skytag.com) or Rainer Brockerhoff's $10 XRay (www.brockerhoff.net) to toggle the visibility bit on the Music folder and the folders within it.

11. When the folders are truly visible, drag the Music folder into iTunes' main library to add the tracks to iTunes.

tip The songs you copied from the iPod will be added to iTunes. If you're the tidy type, before copying those files to iTunes, open iTunes' Preferences window, click the Advanced tab, and make sure the options Keep iTunes Music Folder Organized and Copy File to iTunes Music Folder When Adding to Library are enabled. Enabling these options will organize your Library using iTunes' preferred method.

Windows

At the risk of making my Windows readers feel like second-class citizens, please follow the first three steps outlined in the instructions for Mac users. After you've done that:

1. Double-click the My Computer icon on the desktop.

2. Select your iPod in the window that appears.

3. Choose Tools > Folder Options in the My Computer window.

4. Click the View tab in the Folder Options window that appears.

Figure 7.2
Enable the Show Hidden Files and Folders option to view the invisible iPod_Control folder on your Windows PC.

5. Below the Hidden Files and Folders entry, enable the Show Hidden Files and Folders option (**Figure 7.2**); then click Apply to reveal the hidden files.

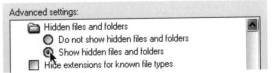

Advanced settings:

📁 Hidden files and folders
  ○ Do not show hidden files and folders
  ◉ Show hidden files and folders
  ☐ Hide extensions for known file types

6. Dismiss the Folder Options windows by clicking the OK button.

7. Double-click the iPod's icon in the My Computer window; then, in the window that opens, double-click the iPod_Control folder.

Inside the iPod_Control folder, you'll find the Device, iTunes, and Music folders, along with some other files.

8. Drag the Music folder to the desktop to copy it to your PC.

9. When the Music folder is on the desktop, right-click the folder, choose Properties from the contextual menu, uncheck the Hidden option in the Attributes area of the General tab, and click Apply.

10. In the Confirm Attributes Change window that appears, make sure that the Apply Changes to This Folder, Subfolders, and Files option is checked, and click OK.

The folder and all the items in it are now visible and can be dragged into the iTunes Library.

note Although the music files bear seemingly incomprehensible four-letter titles (AHLK.m4a, for example) when viewed outside of iTunes, their titles will appear properly once you've brought them into iTunes.

More-refined methods

Scan sites such as hotfiles.com and VersionTracker (http://versiontracker.com), and you'll discover a host of utilities designed to pull media off your iPod and onto your computer. Some of these utilities are more sophisticated than others, allowing you to copy not only the music the iPod carries, but its playlists as well. Here are a few of my favorites.

Macintosh

Whitney Young's free Senuti (www.fadingred.org/ senuti) offers a straightforward interface for moving media off your iPod (**Figure 7.3**). Like similar utilities, it allows you to select tracks and videos on the iPod and then copy them to a location of your choosing. Unlike other utilities, Senuti lets you copy not only videos, single songs, and songs grouped by artist and album, but also complete playlists from the iPod.

Figure 7.3
Senuti's iTunes-like interface.

Windows

Wind Solutions' $20 CopyPod (www.copypod.net)
does much of what Senuti does, but without Senuti's
attractive price. It too features an iPod-like interface
and can copy music as well as video from the iPod to
a Windows PC.

iPodSoft's $20 iGadget (www.ipodsoft.com) can also
move media from the iPod to your PC, exporting
movies, single songs, or playlists. It can also transfer
data to the iPod, such as weather forecasts, local
movie times, driving directions, and RSS news feeds.
This information appears in the iPod's Notes area.

Get the Greatest Charge out of Your iPod

No, I'm not being colloquial. I don't intend to tell
you how to get the greatest thrill out of your iPod,
but how to coax the longest play time from a single
battery charge.

Keep it warm (but not too warm). Lithium-ion
batteries perform at their best when they're oper-
ated at room temperature. If your iPod is cold, warm
it up by putting it under your arm (which, with a
really chilly iPod, is an invigorating way to wake up
in the morning). And keep your iPod out of your car's
hot glove compartment.

Flip on the Hold switch. If you accidentally turn your
iPod on while it's in a pocket, purse, or backpack,
you'll be disappointed hours later when you discover

that its battery has been drained by playing only for itself. An engaged Hold switch will keep this from occurring.

Don't touch it. OK, that's a bit extreme. What I really mean is that every time you press a button, the iPod has to make an additional effort, which drains the battery more quickly.

Turn off EQ and Sound Check, and don't use back-lighting. These extras—particularly backlighting—eat into your battery's charge.

Load your iPod with songs smaller than 9 MB (iPods with hard drives only). The more often your iPod's hard drive spins up, the more quickly its battery is drained. Files that exceed 9 MB force more frequent hard-drive spins. For this reason, you'll get more play time from your iPod if your song files are in the compressed AAC and MP3 formats versus the big ol' AIFF, WAV, and Apple Lossless formats. Flash-based iPods (the nano and shuffle) don't have hard drives, so feel free to feed them large files.

Turn down the brightness control. 5G iPods updated with the latest iPod software include brightness controls. The brighter your iPod's display, the faster your battery drains.

Convert Video for iPod

The iTunes store offers a growing trove of TV shows and movies you can purchase for viewing on your video-capable iPod, but chances are good you have some personal videos you'd like to load onto the device too – either homemade digital video from your camcorder, or possibly from commercial movies you already own and don't care to re-purchase at The Store.

note

A non-lawyer's free legal advice (and you know what that's worth): Copying media you don't own is illegal, whether or not you profit from your efforts; and the legality of duplicating copyrighted DVDs, even those you own, is murky territory. (The law allows you to make a single copy of each DVD for archival purposes; does a copy to your iPod count? Does a copy cease to be archival if you watch it?) Use your own judgment in following the advice in this section.

Rip commercial DVDs

Video-capable iPods recognize two related forms of digital video, generically called H.264 and MPEG-4. Generally speaking, the newer H.264 option is better for iPods; it includes support for high-definition video, and generally yields higher-quality video and smaller file sizes than MPEG-4. To convert commercial DVD video to these formats, you face a couple of challenges — removing the copy protection and then creating a video that works with the iPod. There are tools available for the Mac as well as Windows PCs that can do the job.

Mac users should download Techspansion's free HandBrake Lite (www.isquint.org/handbrakelite). To "rip" a DVD, launch the program, insert a DVD in your drive, and click Open. HandBrake Lite will scan the disc, attempting to locate the disc's main feature, and then present a window that displays a Rip button. Click this button and the program will encode the main feature as an MPEG-4 file, suitable for viewing on your iPod (or a TV attached to it). HandBrake, a more feature rich (though still free) version of the program, let's you muck with the more arcane aspects of video encoding. You can find a copy at http://handbrake.mok.org and a tutorial for using it at http://playlistmag.com/features/2005/12/convertvideo/index.php.

If there was ever a compelling reason to get a Mac, ripping commercial DVDs for iPod use is it. There just isn't an easy way to do this on a Windows PC. Yes, there's a version of HandBrake for Windows (http://www.sr88.co.uk/projects.php) with a graphical user interface (GUI), but as this book goes to press, it doesn't work with copy-protected DVDs. Once you use a utility such as DVDShrink (www.dvdshrink.org) or DVDDecrypter (www.mrbass.org/dvdrip) to remove the copy protection, HandBrake for Windows will convert the resulting video for iPod, but through an interface that is more complicated than HandBrake Lite's. My hope is that by the time you read this, HandBrake's developers will have come up with a GUI as intuitive as the one found in the Mac version of the program.

Convert home video

To convert your unprotected homemade video for iPod use, Apple's $29 QuickTime Pro, which is downloadable for both Mac and Windows from http://www.apple.com/quicktime, is just the ticket.

Open your favorite video clip, choose File > Export, and select the Movie to iPod option from the Export pop-up menu. This creates a H.264 file at a size up to 640-by-480 — a good resolution for TV viewing. Drag the resultant file into your iTunes Library and sync your iPod.

To create smaller files that look good on an iPod but blocky on a TV, Mac users should try Techspansion's free iSquint (www.isquint.com), which produces videos in the iPod's native resolution of 320-by-240.

Shift Your iTunes Library

It may not happen today, tomorrow, or next year, but if you're an iTunes enthusiast, your computer's startup drive will eventually be so choked with media that you won't have room for anything else. When this happens, you'll want to move your iTunes Library to another hard drive. Here's how:

1. Create a new location for your media files—in a folder on an additional internal or external hard drive, for example.

2. Launch iTunes, and choose iTunes > Preferences (Mac) or Edit > Preferences (Windows) to open the iTunes Preferences window.

3. Click the Advanced pane and then the General tab, and click the Change button.

4. In the resulting Change Music Folder Location dialog box, navigate to the new location you just created, and click Choose.

5. In that same Advanced pane, enable the Keep iTunes Music Folder Organized and Copy Files to iTunes Music Folder When Adding to Library options (**FIGURE 7.4**); then click OK to dismiss the Preferences window.

6. Choose Advanced > Consolidate Library.

As the dialog box that appears indicates, this command will copy all your media files to the iTunes Music folder—a version of that Music folder that now exists on another drive.

Figure 7.4
iTunes'
Advanced
preferences
configured for
shifting the
location of your
music library.

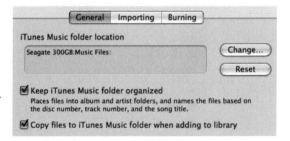

7. Click Consolidate.

iTunes copies not only your files to the destination you designated, but also your Library's playlists. (Ratings will be maintained as well.)

With iTunes 7, you can span an iTunes Library across volumes. To do this, open the Advanced pane of the iTunes Preferences window, select the General tab, click the Change button, and designate a new iTunes Music folder location. With the Copy Files to iTunes Music Folder When Adding to Library option off, iTunes will look to this new folder while also maintaining contact with the old one; you still can play the files from your old iTunes Music folder as well as the new one. When you add new music, it will be added to the new location.

The Bootable iPod

Hypnotize your iPod; ask it to travel back, back, back to its infancy; and it will murmur that long before it learned to carry a tune, it was little more than a removable hard drive. This capability remains, and if you're a Mac user, this is a feature that you can work to your advantage.

In some cases, hard drive–bearing iPods (sorry, no shuffles or iPod nanos) can be configured to boot a Macintosh. I waffle because some iPods will boot some Macs and not others. It's like this:

If you have a PowerPC-based Macintosh (not one with an Intel processor), and your iPod supports FireWire syncing (this includes all hard drive–bearing iPods before the 5G iPod), you can install a copy of Mac OS X on the iPod just as though it were any other external FireWire drive. A 5G iPod won't boot a PowerPC Mac because the PowerPC Mac can't be booted from a USB hard drive.

If you have an Intel-based Macintosh, you can boot it from a 5G iPod if (and only if) you put a compatible version of OS X on that iPod in just the right way. And doing it just the right way means cloning a bootable volume to the iPod with a tool such as the free Carbon Copy Cloner (www.bombich.com). That bootable volume must have a copy of the Mac OS that's compatible with Intel Macs.

And why would you want to create a bootable iPod? The truth is, you may not need to. You may own the one Macintosh in the world that will never, ever suffer from hard-disk corruption and buggy software. For you, having a reliable bootup disk that contains all your troubleshooting utilities isn't necessary.

Or your musical cravings may be so intense that if you can't cram in every minute of the 55.55 days of continuous music that the 80 GB iPod is capable of storing, you'll wind up with a bad case of the heebie-jeebies (or, worse yet, the jim-jams).

I'm not one of these people. Because I troubleshoot Macs for a living, I find the ability to store all the tools I need on such a portable, bootable hard drive to be a real benefit. And although I love music, I hardly find it limiting to store only a few hundred hours of music on my iPod. It's so easy to replace songs on the device with new material that when I get bored with my current selections, I plug the iPod into my computer and dump a different hundred hours of music onto it. My listening needs are met for the next couple of months.

Even if you don't boot from the iPod, there are good reasons to use a portion of it for data storage. When I hit the road, for example, I drop copies of important documents and presentations on my iPod. That way, should my laptop go south, I've still got the files I need to get my work done. An iPod is also a great sneakernet storage device—a handy removable hard drive you can use to transfer large documents from one computer to another when you don't have the ability (or patience) to set up a network.

Spread the Word

If you want to alert your pals to your new favorite podcast, there's no need to send them to the iTunes Store. Just select Podcasts in iTunes' Source list, choose the show title (but not a particular episode) you want to share with your friends, and drag it to your computer's desktop. The title will be turned into a podcast subscription file (with a .pcast extension). Email this file to your nearest and dearest. When they drag the file into iTunes (or double-click it), they'll be subscribed to the podcast that's linked to the file.

iPod shuffle, Autofill, Podcasts, and You

iTunes does its best to cram the most music it can onto an iPod shuffle. For this reason, a shuffle won't play Apple Lossless files, which tend to take up a lot of space; neither will it automatically download AIFF files to the shuffle (though these files will play on the 2G shuffle). Likewise, the Autofill feature that's available when you plug in an iPod shuffle won't add audiobooks or podcasts (which can also be meaty) to a shuffle, even if you've gathered those podcasts into a playlist.

You can, of course, add those files to the shuffle by dragging them to the shuffle entry in iTunes' Source list. Alternatively, if you convert podcasts to a different format—AAC, for example—Autofill will have no objection to pulling them over to the iPod automatically.

To perform that conversion, choose the encoder you'd like to use in the Importing tab of iTunes' Advanced Preferences window; then choose Advanced > Convert Selection to XXX (where XXX is the encoder you've chosen in the Importing tab). With the right configuration—the AAC encoder, using the Spoken Podcast setting from the Setting pop-up menu, for example—you can create files smaller than the originals.

Note that when you convert these files, they'll lose any chapter marks they had, and the podcasts will no longer be bookmarkable. To make a podcast book-markable, select it, choose File > Get Info, click the Options tab, enable the Remember Playback Position option, and click OK.

Add Radio Stations to iTunes

Select the Radio entry in iTunes' Source list, and if your computer is connected to the Internet, you'll discover that you can listen to streaming Internet radio broadcasts in just about every genre imaginable. From all appearances, only Apple can add stations to these radio listings. But appearances can be deceiving; you can add other stations to the iTunes Library and to playlists of your own.

To do so, find a station you want streamed to your computer. The free SHOUTcast (www.shoutcast.com) provides a load of links to streaming stations. Click the link to the station, and download the resulting .pls (playlist) file to your computer. If the playlist doesn't open in iTunes automatically, drag the file into iTunes' main window; it will appear in the iTunes Library as an MPEG audio stream, which you can listen to (**FIGURE 7.5**). Now you can create a new playlist and drag your stations into it, thus giving yourself access to all your custom stations from one location.

Figure 7.5
Streaming
Internet radio
stations in
iTunes.

	Name
1	☑ 🎵 .977 The 80s Channel
2	☑ 🎵 .977 The Hitz Channel
3	☑ 🎵 (#5 – 20/20) CLUB 977 The Hitz Channel (HIGH BANDWIDTH)
4	☑ 🎵 A Classical Concert – Favorites by the great composers – many fro...
5	☑ 🎵 abcrad_kgo_kgo_aac
6	☑ 🎵 CLUB 977 The Hitz Channel (HIGH BANDWIDTH)
7	☑ 🎵 Default stream name
8	☑ 🎵 download.php
9	☑ 🎵 Memories 89 One KCEA–FM
10	☑ 🎵 Mplive Radio
11	☑ 🎵 radioioClassical. Your world. Your station. No boundaries. ©2006 i...
12	☑ 🎵 TSFJAZZ [www.tsfjazz.com] – 96 kbps – canal 2 – 50 slots

Make Allowances

If you're like a lot of iTunes Store customers, you occasionally bust your budget and purchase more music than you should. To help you keep your spending in check, let me show you how to give yourself an iTunes allowance.

As I mentioned in Chapter 4, the iTunes Store allows you to give other users a music allowance—in amounts from $10 to $200—that renews automatically each month. Regrettably, Apple forbids you to create an allowance for the account you've logged in with.

The trick, therefore, is to create an second Apple ID that confers an allowance on your original ID. It works this way:

Launch iTunes, and travel to the iTunes Store via the iTunes Store link. If you're signed into The Store, choose Store > Sign Out. Then choose Store > Sign In (or click the Sign In button in the top-right corner of the iTunes window). In the window that appears, click Create New Account.

In the window that appears next, agree to the license agreement (if you don't, everything stops here), and create a new account on the Step 2 of 3 page. To do so, you need an email address other than the one you used to create your original Apple ID; Apple tracks its users by email address. On the next page, enter your credit-card information, and complete the process.

note You can create up to five Apple IDs with a single credit-card number. Your request to create a sixth account tied to a particular credit-card account will be denied.

After you've signed in with the new account, click the Allowance link on The Store's main page. Navigate through the allowance-creation screens, and enter your original Apple ID as the recipient of the allowance. You'll have the option to start an allowance right now or to have the allowance kick in at the beginning of the next month.

The last step, of course, requires a measure of self-control. When you've used up your monthly allowance, stop buying music!

8

Troubleshooting
Your iPod

I regret to report that—except for you, dear reader, and me—nothing is perfect. No, not even the iPod. Whereas it may tick happily along one day, the next day, its menu structure is a mess; it refuses to start up when you're sure it has a full battery; or when it does start up, it displays an icon indicating that it is feeling far from well.

In this chapter, I'll look at the common maladies that afflict the iPod and what, if anything, you can do about them. I'll also examine the hidden diagnostic screen on click-wheel iPods.

Problems and Solutions

Unlike a computer, which can fail in seemingly countless and creative ways, the iPod exhibits only a few behaviors when it's feeling poorly. Following are the most common problems and (when available) their solutions.

The missing iPod

When you plug your iPod into your Mac or PC, it should make its presence known in short order—appearing in iTunes. If you've configured your iPod to mount as a disk drive, it will also materialize and remain on the Mac's Desktop or within Windows' My Computer window.

If your Macintosh-formatted iPod refuses to mount, restart your Mac while holding down the Shift key. This boots Macs running Mac OS X into Safe Mode. iPods that do not mount otherwise have been known to do so on Macs running in Safe Mode.

If that doesn't do the trick—or if this trick isn't applicable because you're using your iPod with a Windows PC—first reset the iPod. For an iPod shuffle, this entails simply switching the iPod off for 5 seconds. If it's a click-wheel iPod, hold down both the Center and Menu buttons for 6 seconds. For a first-, second-, or third-generation (1G, 2G, or 3G) iPod, plug it into a power outlet, and hold down the Play and Menu buttons for 6 seconds.

If your non-shuffle iPod still won't mount, try forcing it into Disk Mode, as follows: Repeat the reset procedure described above and, when you see the Apple logo on the iPod screen, hold down the Center and Play buttons (click-wheel iPods) or the Previous and Next buttons (1G, 2G, or 3G iPods).

Obviously, none of these techniques is a good long-term solution, as you don't want to restart your Mac in Safe Mode, reset the iPod, or force it into Disk Mode whenever you sync it. An iPod that won't mount is one that should be restored with the latest iPod software, which is accessible through the iPod's Summary tab in iTunes.

PC laptops may not recognize a connected iPod if the computer is configured to turn off power to the USB ports to conserve power. To prevent this from happening, choose Start > Control Panel, double-click the System icon, click the Hardware tab, and click the Device Manager button. In the resulting window, locate the Universal Serial Bus entry in the list of devices, and click the plus sign (+) next to the entry to expand it. Double-click each USB Root Hub entry, click the Power Management tab (*phew, almost finished...*), disable the Allow the Computer to Turn off This Device to Save Power option, click OK to dismiss the window, and restart the computer.

The confused iPod

Clues that your iPod is confused include the absence of videos, playlists, artists, and songs that used to be there; the failure of the iPod to boot beyond the Apple logo; and the appearance of a folder icon with an exclamation point. In the following sections, I'll look at these scenarios (which don't apply to the iPod shuffle because it isn't complex enough to get confused in these ways).

Absence of items

While I was attempting to use a Macintosh-formatted standard iPod on a Windows PC, my PC crashed, and when I unplugged the iPod, its playlists were missing. I could still play music from the iPod through the Songs screen, but things were not right.

In an attempt to restore a sense of sanity to my iPod, I tried these remedies:

1. Reset the iPod (again, for click-wheel iPods, press and hold Select and Menu for 6 seconds; for 1G, 2G, and 3G iPods, plug into a power source and then press and hold Play and Menu for 6 seconds).

   Resetting the iPod is similar to pushing the Reset switch on your computer; it forces the iPod to restart and (ideally) get its little house in order. In this case, the iPod remained confused.

2. Restore the iPod.

If resetting doesn't work, or if your iPod can't seem to find its operating system (it displays a folder icon with an exclamation point), there's nothing else for it than to restore the iPod to its original factory state—meaning that all the data on it is removed, and the iPod's firmware is updated.

To restore the iPod with iTunes 7 or later, just plug the iPod into your computer's powered USB port (or FireWire port for older iPods), and click the iPod's icon in the iTunes Source list. In the Summary tab, you'll see the option to Restore the iPod (**FIGURE 8.1**). Click the Restore button. The iPod will be reformatted and, with just a little luck, will perform in a more acceptable manner.

Figure 8.1 The Restore button, located in the Summary tab of iTunes' iPod panel.

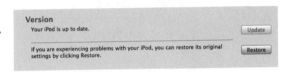

When you double-click your iPod's icon on the Mac's Desktop or in Windows' My Computer window after the restore, you'll see that the device contains only the Calendars, Contacts, and (on 3G and click-wheel iPods) Notes folders, with the sample contacts and Notes instructions supplied by Apple.

To put your songs back on the iPod, just sync the iPod with iTunes in your preferred manner. After a restore, the iPod will revert to the default setting, which is to be updated automatically by iTunes. Just as you were when you first plugged your brand-new iPod into your computer, you'll be asked how you'd like to sync your iPod before iTunes takes it upon itself to move media onto your iPod.

note On very rare occasions, restoring the iPod on a computer platform other than the one you usually use can make the iPod more cooperative. In other words, if restoring the iPod on a Macintosh doesn't work, try restoring it on a Windows PC (or vice versa).

Failure to boot

There are a few possible reasons why an iPod might not boot beyond the Apple logo—some benign and others not so.

The Hold switch is on. Go ahead and smack yourself in the head (and then breathe a sigh of relief) if your iPod won't start up because the Hold switch is engaged.

Drained battery. Among the most benign problems is an iPod battery that's drained (though not dead; I'll discuss dead iPod batteries in the "Assault on Batteries" sidebar later in this chapter). If the iPod is functioning normally otherwise, switching it on when its battery is very nearly drained causes a low-battery icon to appear on the display. If the battery is completely drained, the iPod can't even muster the energy to display this icon; the screen remains black, and the drive refuses to spin up. Plug your iPod into the power adapter or your computer, and let it charge. If everything's hunky-dory after that, pat yourself on the back for a job well done.

If you've plugged the iPod's data/power cable into a computer that isn't currently charging it—one that's turned off or asleep, for example—unplug the iPod. Some people have reported that when the iPod is plugged in but isn't being charged, its power can dissipate quickly.

If your computer won't charge your iPod, it's possible that something is wrong with its USB or FireWire port. Try plugging your iPod into a different port or power adapter. If the iPod charges, it's time to cock a suspicious eyebrow at your computer.

In some rare cases, the battery may not be charged enough for the iPod to be reset. If you've tried other solutions and failed, unplug the iPod from a power supply for 24 hours; then plug it into a power source and attempt to reset it.

Songs skip

Songs played on the iPod may skip for several reasons, which include:

Large song files. Large song files (long symphonic movements or those endless Grateful Dead jams, for example) don't play particularly well with the 32 MB RAM buffer on iPods with hard drives. (The 60 GB and 80 GB fifth-generation [5G] iPods have a larger RAM buffer and do better with long files.) Large song files race through the RAM buffer, requiring the iPod to access the hard drive more often. This situation can lead to skipping if the iPod is pulling the song almost directly from the hard drive. If possible, reduce the sizes of files by employing greater compression, or chop really long files (such as audio-books) into pieces.

Damaged file. A damaged song file may skip. If you find that the same song skips every time you play it—and other songs seem to play back with no problem—go back to the source of the song (an audio CD, for example), rip the song again, and replace the copy on the iPod with the newly ripped version.

iPod that needs to be reset. Yes, an iPod that needs to be reset may cause songs to skip. (Refer to "The confused iPod" earlier in this chapter for instructions.)

iPod that needs to be restored. If a reset won't do the trick, make sure that all the data on your iPod is backed up, and restore the iPod from the iPod panel's Summary tab. (Instructions for doing so are in "The confused iPod" earlier in this chapter.)

Unpleasant sound as the hard drive spins up

This symptom appeared in some early releases of the fourth-generation (4G) iPods and a very few color iPods. Typically, iPods with this problem will make noise through the Headphone port whenever the hard drive spins up. Static accompanies the first couple of seconds of songs played after the iPod spins up.

This appears to be a grounding issue that makes itself known only when you've plugged in headphones whose audio connector bears a metal base that comes into contact with the iPod's case. This metal-to-metal contact transmits this sound through your headphones. To troubleshoot the issue, place a small plastic washer on the post of any affected headphones.

The really confused iPod

Your iPod may be so confused that it won't mount on your Mac's Desktop or in Windows' My Computer window and can't be restored. Follow these steps to mount the iPod:

1. Connect a 1G, 2G, or 3G iPod to a built-in FireWire port on your computer (rather than an unpowered FireWire port on a PC Card or a USB 2.0 port, for example). Because the click-wheel iPods can be powered via a USB 2.0 connection, feel free to use such a connection with your Mac or Windows PC.

2. Reset the 1G, 2G, or 3G iPod by holding down the Play and Menu buttons for 6 seconds. Reset the click-wheel iPods by holding down Select and Menu for 6 seconds.

3. When you see the Apple logo, hold down the Previous and Next buttons on the first three generations of the iPod until you see a message that reads "Do not disconnect." On the click-wheel iPods, hold down Select and Play.

   The key combination outlined in step 2 resets the iPod much like pressing the Reset switch on a PC or Mac resets the computer. The second key combination forces the iPod into Disk Mode—a mode that will help your computer recognize and mount the iPod.

   With luck, your iPod should appear on the Mac's Desktop or in Windows' My Computer window. Then you should be able to restore it.

Secret Button Combinations

By pressing the proper combination of buttons on the iPod's face, you can force the device to reset, enter Disk Mode, scan its hard disk for damage, and perform a series of diagnostic tests. Here are those combinations and the wonders they perform.

When you reset your iPod, your data remains intact, but the iPod restores the factory settings. This technique reboots the iPod and is helpful when your iPod is locked up.

Click-wheel iPods: Plug the iPod into a powered device (the Apple iPod Power Adapter, an auto adapter, or a built-in FireWire port) or a high-powered USB 2.0 port; then hold down the Center and Menu buttons for 6 seconds.

iPod shuffle: Disconnect the shuffle from your computer, move the power switch to the Off position, wait 5 seconds, and switch it back to On (or to the Play in Order or Shuffle position for the 1G iPod shuffle). (Yes, resetting a shuffle is really nothing more than turning it off and on again.)

First three generations of the full-size iPod: Plug the iPod into a powered FireWire device (the Apple iPod Power Adapter, an auto adapter, or a built-in FireWire port), and hold down Play and Menu for 6 seconds.

DISK MODE

Use this technique when you need to mount your iPod on a Mac with an unpowered FireWire card (a FireWire PC Card in your older PowerBook, for example) or on a PC with a similarly unpowered FireWire or USB 2.0 connection.

Click-wheel iPods: Reset the iPod. When the Apple logo appears, hold down the Center and Play buttons.

First three generations of the full-size iPod: Reset the iPod. When you see the Apple logo, hold down the Previous and Next buttons.

continues on next page

DISK SCAN

Use this method to check the integrity of your iPod's hard drive. This test can take 15 to 20 minutes, so be patient. Be sure to plug your iPod into the power adapter when you perform this test so that the iPod doesn't run out of juice before the scan is complete. If the scan shows no problems, a check mark appears over the disk icon on the first three generations of the full-size iPod.

First three generations of the full-size iPod: Reset the iPod. At the Apple logo, hold down the Previous, Next, Center, and Menu buttons. An animated icon of a disc and magnifying glass with a progress bar below it appears.

Click-wheel iPods: These iPods don't offer a button combination to scan the hard drive. Rather, you must access this function through the iPod's Diagnostic screen (which I explain at great length in the "Doing Diagnostics" sidebar later in this chapter).

DIAGNOSTIC MODE

See the "Doing Diagnostics" sidebar later in this chapter for more details.

Click-wheel iPods: Reset the iPod. At the Apple logo, hold down the Center and Previous buttons.

First three generations of the full-size iPod: Reset the iPod. At the Apple logo, hold down the Center, Previous, and Next buttons.

The frozen iPod

Just like a computer, the iPod can freeze from time to time. To thaw it, attach your iPod to a power source—the power adapter, a powered FireWire port, or a computer's high-powered USB 2.0 port—and, on the first three generations of the iPod, hold down the Play and Menu buttons for 6 seconds. For click-wheel iPods, hold down the Center and Menu buttons for the same 6 seconds.

Failure to charge

There are several reasons why an iPod might not charge. They include all of the following:

A sleeping computer. The iPod may not charge when it's attached to a sleeping computer. (Some sleeping computers will charge an iPod; others won't.) If you suspect that a sleepy computer is the problem, wake up your computer if you want the iPod to charge.

The wrong cable. Remember, a USB 2.0 connection carries no power to 3G iPods (though it does to click-wheel iPods). To charge your 1G, 2G, or 3G iPod on a Windows PC, you must plug your iPod into a powered FireWire port or the iPod's power adapter.

More than one FireWire device on the chain. Although you can chain multiple FireWire devices, doing so with an iPod isn't such a good idea. To begin with, a FireWire device on the chain before the iPod (a hard drive, for example) may be hogging all the power. Second, there have been reports of iPods that got corrupted when they were left on a chain with other FireWire devices. To be safe rather than sorry, don't put the iPod on a FireWire chain. If you must use multiple FireWire devices, purchase a powered FireWire hub (which costs between $45 and $65).

A frozen iPod. An iPod that's frozen won't charge. Reset the iPod with the instructions given in "The confused iPod" earlier in the chapter.

Assault on Batteries

There's been a great deal of hoopla surrounding the iPod's battery—specifically, how long it should last and why it's so darned difficult to replace. Let's set the record straight.

All iPods carry a lithium-ion (Li-ion) battery. Theoretically, Li-ion batteries, by their very nature, can be fully charged up to 500 times. In actual practice, your iPod's battery will put up with between 300 and 450 complete charges before it gives up the ghost.

This is all well and good if you charge your iPod once a week or so. But if you use your iPod constantly—and, thus, fully charge it four or five times a week—you'll discover that after about a year and a half, it's kaput.

As you might imagine, those who've seen their iPods kick the bucket after a year and a half have been less than joyous about it. After all, a device you paid several hundred dollars for should have a longer shelf life than a Twinkie. Adding to this unhappiness was Apple's policy of charging $255 to replace the iPod.

Apple and some third-party battery vendors got hip to the situation as the first couple of revisions of the iPod began to go south due to dead batteries.

If your iPod is more than a year old, and it fails to hold a charge, Apple will replace it with another "functionally equivalent new, used, or refurbished iPod" for $59 (plus $6.95 for shipping). That "functionally equivalent" stuff means that you won't get back the same iPod that you send in. You'll get one from the "good pile" that has the same capacity and is of the same generation as the one you sent in. If you send in an engraved iPod, Apple will take the back plate off your iPod and put it on the replacement iPod. For more details, visit http://depot.info.apple.com/ipod.

continues on next page

If you're mechanically inclined, it's fairly easy to replace the battery in a 1G or 2G iPod. But newer models are tougher nuts to crack. The iPod mini is particularly difficult to open, for example, and the 3G iPod includes a thin cable that's attached to both the motherboard and a connector on the back plate; open it the wrong way, and you could break the cable, which will destroy your iPod. For this reason, it's safest to have a professional install your new battery. iPodResQ (www.ipodresq.com) offers a battery-replacement service for $54, and OtherWorldComputing (http://eshop.macsales.com) will install a Newer Technology battery for the price of the part plus a $39 service charge. A Google search will turn up any number of companies willing to sell you a replacement iPod battery, plus the tools and instructions necessary to open the iPod.

A faulty cable. Cables break. Try a different data/power cable, just in case yours has gone the way of the dodo.

A faulty computer port. It's possible that the FireWire or USB 2.0 port on your computer has given up the ghost. Try charging the iPod from the Apple iPod Power Adapter.

A funky power adapter. The Apple iPod Power Adapter could also be bad. Attempt to charge your iPod from your computer.

A faulty data/power port on the iPod. This problem is more common on 1G and 2G iPods than it is on later iPods. As you plug and unplug the FireWire cable from the iPod's FireWire port on these old iPods, it's possible to put too much stress on the internal connectors that deliver power to your iPod's FireWire port, breaking the bond between those connectors and your iPod's motherboard.

A dead battery. Like all lithium-ion batteries, the iPod's battery is good for 300 to 500 full charges. When you've exhausted those charges, your iPod needs a new battery. See the sidebar "Assault on Batteries" for more details.

Broken iPod. iPods occasionally break. If none of these solutions brings your iPod back from its never-ending slumber, it may need to be replaced. Contact Apple at http://depot.info.apple.com/ipod.

The broken iPod

It's a machine, and regrettably, machines break. If none of these solutions brings your iPod back from the dead, it may need to be repaired. If you live near an Apple Store or another outfit that sells iPods, take it in. If such a trip is impractical, contact Apple at http://depot.info.apple.com/ipod for instructions on how to have your iPod serviced.

When you take a misbehaving iPod to a Genius at the Apple Store, said Genius will run a couple of tests on it. If it fails to respond, the Genius may try to restore it (which is why you should always have a backup of your music and data).

If that doesn't work, and your iPod is under warranty, you'll probably get a replacement on the spot (provided that Apple still sells the same iPod model, with the same storage capacity, as the one you bring in). If you have an iPod under warranty, and Apple's changed the iPod line—you've got a 40 GB 5G iPod, for example, and Apple sells 5G iPods only in 30 GB and 80 GB capacities—Apple will arrange to get you an iPod of similar capacity. (Sorry, but you're unlikely to get the next size up, even though it sells for the same price you paid for yours.) If the iPod is out of warranty, you'll have to pay for the repair.

Doing Diagnostics

Ever wonder what Apple technicians do when they want to test an iPod? Just as you can, they reset the iPod, and when they see the Apple logo, they hold down the Center, Previous, and Next buttons on the first three generations of the full-size iPod, and the Center and Previous buttons on click-wheel iPods.

When you do this, you may hear a chirp. (Not all iPods chirp.) Release the buttons, and you'll see a screen of text that eventually resolves to a list of tests.

In the big ol' *Secrets of the iPod and iTunes*, I detail each of these tests. I don't have the room to do so here, but I can give you the gist.

Most of these tests take a gander at the iPod's controllers and internal components: the hard drive, display, SDRAM chip, battery, and Headphone and Dock Connector ports. For most people, these tests are nothing more than a curiosity, which is one reason why Apple refuses to talk about the Diagnostic screen.

If you have a hard disk–based iPod (any model with a display, except the nano), these tests can tell you whether your iPod's hard drive is on the way out. How you access the hard-drive test depends on which iPod model you have.

5G iPod: Reset the iPod by holding down the Center and Menu buttons for 6 seconds. When you see the Apple logo, hold down

continues on next page

the Center and Previous buttons until you hear a beep and the screen lights up. You'll see a SRV Diag Boot screen. Press Menu to enter the Manual Test screen. Hold down Next until the pointer reaches IO; then press the Center button. Hold down Next until you reach HardDrive; then press the Center button. The next screen shows just two entries: HDSpecs and HDSMARTData. Hold down Next to advance to HDSMARTData; then press the Center button. In a couple of seconds, you'll see a SMART Data screen that provides you a few statistics but no actual hard-drive test. The entries you want to pay attention to are Reallocs and Pending Sectors. Ideally, both of these will read 0. Reallocs indicates the number of bad sectors on the hard drive that were reallocated; lots of bad blocks is not a good thing. Pending Sectors means that the self-running maintenance tests have found this many bad sectors on the drive but have yet to reallocate them. Any figure shown here other than 0 isn't good.

Pre-5G color iPods and iPod mini: Reset the iPod by holding down the Center and Menu buttons for 6 seconds. When you see the Apple logo, hold down the Center and Previous buttons until you see the Apple logo reverse and the iPod blink. When the Diagnostic screen appears, hold down Next until IO is highlighted; then press the Center button. Hold down Next until HardDrive is selected; then press the Center button again, and hold down Next to select HDScan. Plug the iPod into a power source before running the scan, as it will drain the battery quickly. If the iPod's hard drive is OK, you will be taken back to the HardDrive screen.

4G iPod: Reset the iPod by holding down the Center and Menu buttons for 6 seconds. When you see the Apple logo, hold down the Center and Previous buttons until you see the Apple logo reverse and the iPod blink. Let go; then hold down Next to scroll down the list of tests until you select HDD Scan. Press the Center button to begin the test. Be sure that the iPod is plugged into a power source during this test, as it will drain a battery quickly.

continues on next page

If your iPod's hard drive is OK, you'll eventually see HDD Pass. And if it's not OK? Beats me—Apple won't talk about it, and I've never had a hard drive fail. My best guess is that if you see something other than HDD Pass, there's a problem that warrants a peek by Apple's techs.

iPod nano: This iPod has no hard drive, but you can check the flash memory on 1G models. Enter Diagnostic Mode as you do on a color iPod or mini, and press the Next button to select FlashScan. If the iPod passes, you'll see Test OK. The 2G nano has many diagnostic routines, including a mildly entertaining LCD-display check, but it lacks the FlashScan test.

To exit Diagnostic Mode, reset the iPod by holding down the Center and Menu buttons for 6 seconds.

Thank You

As thanks for purchasing this book, I'd like to give you a little something to put on your iPod. That little something is Of Eve, a solo piano album I recorded some years ago.

The music on Of Eve belongs to me, but you're welcome to download and place it on your computer and iPod for your personal listening pleasure. You may not, however, use this music in a public broadcast or for any commercial purposes without my permission.

You can find your copy here: www.peachpit.com/ ipodsecrets.

I hope you enjoy it.

Index